January 6
and the Politics
of History

HISTORY
IN THE HEADLINES

January 6
and the Politics
of History

EDITED BY Jim Downs

The University of Georgia Press   *Athens*

Set in Garamond Premier Pro and ITC Franklin Gothic
Printed and bound by Sheridan Books
The paper in this book meets the guidelines for
permanence and durability of the Committee on
Production Guidelines for Book Longevity of the
Council on Library Resources.

Most University of Georgia Press titles are
available from popular e-book vendors.

Printed in the United States of America
28   27   26   25   24   P   5   4   3   2   1

Library of Congress Cataloging-in-Publication Data

Names: Downs, Jim, 1973– editor.
Title: January 6 and the politics of history / edited by Jim Downs.
Description: Athens : The University of Georgia Press, [2024] |
Series: History in the headlines | Includes bibliographical references.
Identifiers: LCCN 2023040861 | ISBN 9780820364056 (hardback) |
   ISBN 9780820364049 (paperback) | ISBN 9780820364063 (epub)|
   ISBN9780820364070 (pdf)
Subjects: LCSH: Capitol Riot, Washington, D.C., 2021. |
   Radicalism—Washington (D.C.)—History—21st century. |
   Political violence—Washington (D.C.)—History—21st century. |
   United States—Politics and government—2017–2021. |
   Riots—Washington (D.C.)—History—21st century. |
   Domestic terrorism—United States—History—21st century. |
   Trump, Donald, 1946– | Presidents—United States—Election—2020. |
   White supremacy movements—United States—History—21st century. |
   Paramilitary forces—United States—History—21st century.
Classification: LCC E915 .J356 2024 | DDC 973.933—dc23
LC record available at https://lccn.loc.gov/2023040861

For Elizabeth Cooper-Mullin, whose commitment to teach about the past is changing the present and inspiring the future.

Contents

Acknowledgments

This book would not be possibly without the generous support and wise counsel of my series coeditor Catherine Clinton, who arranged for us to meet in September 2021 at the Harvard Club in New York City, where the conversation took place. Catherine not only made room and meal reservations, but she also bought covid-19 tests and administered them to everyone. During the early stages of developing the concept for this book, she helped with the proposal and offered insightful and incisive suggestions as the production process unfolded. In the final stages of production, she provided a very close reading of the conversation and added useful annotations that provided vital context.

Taylor Pratt served as the research assistant for this book. She was responsible for recording, transcribing, and providing the first edit of the manuscript. Her efforts were herculean the day of the recording, and I am deeply grateful for her enthusiastic commitment to this project.

I am deeply grateful to Joanne B. Freeman, Elizabeth Hinton, Jill Lepore, Stephanie McCurry, William Sturkey, and Julian Zelizer, who lent their expertise, insight, and, most of all, time to make this book possible. Special thanks to the authors of the op-eds, who all graciously granted permissions to reprint their important interventions.

Thanks to Mick Gusinde-Duffy, our editor at UGA Press, whose patience and good cheer helped to get this book across the finish line.

This book is dedicated to my former student, Elizabeth Cooper-Mullin, who I met my first day of teaching as a professor in 2006, which was also her first day of college. Over the last sixteen years, I have watched her grow as a brilliant thinker, a devoted teacher, and a dedicated student of history, who still gets excited by the prospect of new ideas. I hope this book inspires her as much as she has inspired me.

Jim Downs
Cambridge, Mass.
December 2022

January 6
and the Politics
of History

Introduction

This is an introduction to a conversation among historians Joanne B. Freeman, Elizabeth Hinton, Jill Lepore, Stephanie McCurry, William Sturkey, and Julian Zelizer about January 6. This is not an explanation that charts the causes, ramifications, or significance of the attack on the U.S. Capitol. This is, however, a rare opportunity to catch, in real time, how historians grapple with an event and how they try to piece together a narrative. Journalism is often considered to be the first draft of history, but this conversation is the first book by a group of historians about January 6.

A later generation of historians will indeed write copious studies about January 6, connecting the missing dots and interpreting the mountains of still growing evidence. This volume offers something else—an opportunity to explore how historians approach a question and how they attempt to place the past and present in dialogue. As the conversation shows, historical thinking has both benefits and limitations. Historical analysis provides context, but it also acknowledges how January 6 was unprecedented. The past is not just a menu of events that easily provides antecedents to the present. History isn't even about the past; as the distinguished historian Ira Berlin wrote, "It is about arguments we have about the past. And because it is about arguments that we have, it is about us."[1]

---

1   Ira Berlin, *The Long Emancipation: The Demise of Slavery in the United States* (Cambridge: Harvard University Press, 2015), 1.

Throughout the conversation, the historians wrestled with the question of when the timeline of January 6 begins. Do we trace the events of January 6, as Stephanie McCurry suggested, to the murderous outcome of Reconstruction, or is there a more recent starting place in the backlash against COVID-19 lockdowns and the Black Lives Matters protests, as Elizabeth Hinton posited? Or is the root of January 6 part of the long history of white mob violence, which led to events like the Wilmington uprising in 1898, as William Sturkey explained? Or does the starting point begin with shifts that have been taking place within the Republican Party in the last few decades, as Julian Zelizer claimed? Or did January 6 simply result from President Donald Trump's December 20, 2020 tweet, in which he contested the results of the election: "Statistically impossible to have lost the 2020 Election. Big protest in D.C. on January 6th. Be there, will be wild"?[2]

Maybe it is all these reasons or none of them. While historians may debate these starting points, and even add a score of others to consider, this volume invites students, scholars, and the public to listen in on how historians grapple with the chronology that led to January 6.

Catching historians in real time also highlights how historians' choice of a single word can shape how they narrate the past. What do we call January 6? A coup or a revolution? A protest or an act of sedition? Less than forty-eight hours after January 6, Jill Lepore first raised this question in an article ("What Should We Call the Sixth of January?") that she published in the *New Yorker* and that is republished here. Lepore eventually settled on referring to January 6

2   Tom Dreisbach, "How Trump's 'Will Be Wild!' Tweet Drew Rioters to the Capitol on January 6," NPR, July 13, 2022.

as an "insurrection," but as she and others explore in this discussion, one word can radically change how we interpret January 6.

The questions of what caused January 6, what events precipitated it, and what effects it will have, get at the very heart of historical practice. It is not surprising that the conversation shifted halfway through to the objective of historical scholarship as the group grappled with what scholars have referred to as "the useable past." Do historians write books for other historians, or do they write for the public? Based on her work as a cohost of the *Now and Then* podcast, award-winning historian Joanne Freeman outlined why she feels an urgency to provide historical context to the public. As she explains, "I put the energy into [podcasts and webcasts] because it feels to me people fundamentally don't understand a lot of really basic things, and aren't going to listen to it coming to them as a lesson. But if you put the information out there in an inviting voice, some people actually might hear it."

Freeman also perceptively noted that most times when journalists contact historians about the past to frame a current event, they interview them to gather information rather than ask them to testify.

A debate then broke out about whether the lack of historians in the media resulted from historians' inability to make their scholarship legible to a broader public or if larger market forces prevented historians from breaking into the media. If it's the latter, then is it historians' responsibly to conduct research and write books and, in so doing, provide what Stephanie McCurry called the "raw material" for journalists to cull for their own publications? Jill Lepore pushed back against this idea and added that historians began to retreat from public debates in the aftermath of the Vietnam War.

This exchange was necessary. Typically, public engagement has been treated as an aspiration, a truism, or as an honorific bestowed upon historians who have reached a level of stature that makes their research important to the public, but this urgent conversation interrogated both the possibilities and limitations of historical scholarship—and it even addressed the explosive debates surrounding the 1619 Project, a long form journalism enterprise spearheaded by Pulitzer Prize winner Nikole Hannah Jones in 2019 that emphasized the four hundredth year anniversary of the date when the first enslaved Africans arrived to Virginia. Hannah Jones insists that 1619 ought to have the same historical significance as 1776, which has sparked serious debate about the nation's origins.

This conversation then became a meta reflection on the historian as a public intellectual. What are historians' roles during a crisis? Can they contribute anything of value to the discussion? Should they be hesitant about drawing parallels and analogies? And how should these considerations determine their engagement with the public?

This discussion embodied the objective of the History in the Headlines series. It not only explored the politics and polemics surrounding January 6, but it also investigated how and why we write history. Within days of January 6, several historians fired off opinion pieces in the nation's leading newspapers. None of them were sanguine. In keeping with the mission of this series, this volume includes a "Top Ten Articles" section written by historians following January 6, including essays by award-winning historians David Blight and Karen Cox, who each connected Donald Trump's presidency to the rise of right-wing extremist movements after the Civil War. Building on those interventions, Kathleen Belew penned an incisive essay, "Militia Groups Were Hiding in Plain Sight on

January 6," on the one-year anniversary of January 6. Her work was also cited by Elizabeth Hinton and Stephanie McCurry during the conversation.

Like the roundtable discussion, these opinion pieces catch historians in real time, assessing the present in the context of the past. As I write this introduction, many questions about January 6 remain—most notably about President Trump's involvement in fueling the violence. Scores of history books will invariably be written about Trump, the Republican Party, and the threats to democracy, but this volume is less interested in offering a comprehensive history of January 6 and more interested in exploring the presence of history of the headlines.

The idea for this volume developed in the immediate aftermath of January 6. The soonest we were able to convene for an in-person conversation was September 17, 2021 in New York City, which was one of the first times many of us had gathered in a public space since the outbreak of the COVID-19 pandemic. (We required all participants to be vaccinated and conducted on-site testing the day of the event.) The participates were, in turn, selected due to their proximity to New York City as well as their areas of specialization.

Early America: Jill Lepore
Early Republic: Joanne B. Freeman
Nineteenth Century: Stephanie McCurry
Twentieth Century and Civil Rights: William Sturkey
African American History and Social Movements: Elizabeth Hinton
Twentieth-Century Politics: Julian E. Zelizer

Since we met in New York City, we selected contributors who could easily get to the city during the pandemic, but we sought diversity of opinion in other ways—particularly in terms of race, gender, and generation. We wanted a mix of scholars from various ranks and ages to be in conversation.

Having the conversation in September meant that it took place before a Congressional Select Committee held hearings pertaining to the following:

> Whereas January 6, 2021, was one of the darkest days of our democracy, during which insurrectionists attempted to impede Congress's Constitutional mandate to validate the presidential election and launched an assault on the United States Capitol Complex that resulted in multiple deaths, physical harm to over 140 members of law enforcement, and terror and trauma among staff, institutional employees, press, and Members;
>
> Whereas, on January 27, 2021, the Department of Homeland Security issued a National Terrorism Advisory System Bulletin that due to the "heightened threat environment across the United States," in which "some ideologically-motivated violent extremists with objections to the exercise of governmental authority and the presidential transition, as well as other perceived grievances fueled by false narratives, could continue to mobilize to incite or commit violence."[3]

As part of the "Top Ten Articles," we have included three articles about the hearings from Heather Cox Richardson's daily *Letters from an American Series*, which has become a national sensation. Richardson, who appeared in the second volume of the History in the Headlines series on voter suppression, is an astute historian who provides daily historical assessments of current events. Her

3   U.S. House of Representatives, https://january6th-benniethompson.house .gov/about.https://january6th-benniethompson.house.gov/about Retrieved on July 24https://january6th-benniethompson.house.gov/about Retrieved on July 24https://january6th-benniethompson.house.gov/about Retrieved on July 24

letters offer insight into the period after the roundtable conversation took place.

The hearings have generated reams of testimonies, introduced a whole new set of historical actors, and exposed shocking evidence that will keep future generations of historians busy. This book is historians' first draft in trying to make sense of January 6 and an unprecedented collective account of how we write history.

Roundtable
on January 6 and the Politics of History

September 17, 2021   *New York City*

MODERATOR

Jim Downs is the Gilder Lehrman–National Endowment for the Humanities Professor of Civil War–era Studies and History at Gettysburg College. He is the author of *Maladies of Empire: How Colonialism, Slavery, and War Transformed Medicine*; *Sick from Freedom: African American Sickness and Suffering during the Civil War and Reconstruction*; and *Stand By Me: The Forgotten History of Gay Liberation*. He has edited six anthologies, including *Beyond Freedom: Disrupting the History of Emancipation*, coedited with David Blight. He has published essays in *The Atlantic*, the *New Yorker*, the *Washington Post*, the *New York Times*, *Vice*, and *Slate*, among other publications. He is the editor of *Civil War History* and a partner at History Studio.

PANELISTS

Joanne B. Freeman is a professor of history at Yale. She specializes in the politics and political culture of the revolutionary and early national periods of American history. She earned her PhD at the University of Virginia. Her book *Affairs of Honor: National*

Politics in the New Republic won the Best Book award from the Society of Historians of the Early American Republic and her edited volume, *Alexander Hamilton: Writings,* was one of *Atlantic Monthly's* "best books" of 2001. Her most recent book, *The Field of Blood: Violence in Congress and the Road to Civil War*, was named a *New York Times* Notable Book of 2018.

Elizabeth Hinton is professor of history, African American studies, and law at Yale University. Hinton's past and current scholarship provides a deeper grasp of the persistence of poverty, urban violence, and racial inequality in the United States. She is the author of *From the War on Poverty to the War on Crime: The Making of Mass Incarceration in America* and, most recently, *America on Fire: The Untold History of Police Violence and Black Rebellion Since the 1960s.* Hinton's articles and op-eds can be found in the pages of *Nature, Science,* the *Journal of American History,* the *Journal of Urban History,* the *New York Times, The Atlantic,* the *Boston Review, The Nation,* and *Time.* Hinton also coedited *The New Black History: Revisiting the Second Reconstruction* with the late historian Manning Marable.

Jill Lepore is the David Woods Kemper '41 Professor of American History at Harvard University. She is also a staff writer at *the New Yorker,* and the host of the podcast *The Last Archive.* Her many books include *These Truths: A History of the United States.*

Stephanie McCurry is the R. Gordon Hoxie Professor of American History in Honor of Dwight D. Eisenhower at Columbia University. She teaches and writes about the nineteenth-century United States, the Civil War and emancipation, and women's and gender history. She is the author of three prizewinning books:

Masters of Small Worlds: Yeoman Households, Gender Relations and the Political Culture of the Antebellum South Carolina Low Country; Confederate Reckoning: Power and Politics in the Civil War South, which was a finalist for the Pulitzer Prize; and *Women's War: Fighting and Surviving the American Civil War*. She is currently writing a book about the process of reconstructing the United States in the aftermath of the American Civil War. Told as an epic human drama, it focuses on the explosive tension between dispossession and possession unleased by defeat, emancipation, and military occupation and seeks its measure in intimate relations as well as public life.

William Sturkey is an associate professor of history at the University of Pennsylvania, where his research and teaching focuses on the history of race in the American South. He is the author of *Hattiesburg: An American City in Black and White* and coeditor of *To Write in the Light of Freedom: The Newspapers of the 1964 Mississippi Freedom Schools*.

Julian E. Zelizer has been among the pioneers in the revival of American political history and is a *New York Times* best-selling author. He is the Malcolm Stevenson Forbes Class of 1941 Professor of History and Public Affairs at Princeton University and a CNN political analyst and regular guest on NPR's *Here and Now*. He is the award-winning author or editor of twenty-five books, including *The Fierce Urgency of Now: Lyndon Johnson, Congress, and the Battle for the Great Society*, the winner of the D.B. Hardeman Prize for the best book on Congress; *Fault Lines: A History of the United States Since 1974* (coauthored with Kevin M. Kruse); and *Burning Down the House: Newt Gingrich, the Fall of a Speaker, and the Rise of the New Republican Party*. The *New York Times* named the latter as an Editor's Choice and one of the 100 Notable Books of 2020. His most recent books are *Abraham Joshua Heschel: A Life of Radical Amazement*, *The Presidency of Donald J. Trump: A First Historical Assessment*, which he edited, and *Myth America: Historians Take on the Biggest Lies and Legends about Our Past*, coedited with Kevin M. Kruse. Zelizer, who has published over twelve hundred op-eds, has received fellowships from the Brookings Institution, the Guggenheim Foundation, the Russell Sage Foundation, the New York Historical Society, and New America.

JIM DOWNS: Where were you when you first heard about the uprising on January 6? And what were your initial reactions?

JULIAN E. ZELIZER: I'll start. I had just recorded a show for CNN for Fareed Zakaria on the history of the Republican Party and how extremism, since the 1980s, had gradually taken hold of the party. And so I was in some studio downtown, one of these old automobile places temporarily converted into a television set. I left at around noon. And I was just in the Uber when they called for me and I was watching what was happening in Washington through Twitter. I turned on one of the television stations on my phone to see a longer feed. I was literally watching some of what we had spoken about on the show—the radicalization of the conservative movement—unfold before my eyes. And it was really upsetting. That was my response as the enormity of what was going to happen became very clear. And I was texting my wife, Meg Jacobs, about what was going on. She was also watching it on TV.

JOANNE B. FREEMAN: I think, in my case, I saw a reference to it. I was at home. And I saw something going on clearly at the Capitol, and turned on the TV, and went to social media, and was processing. I was having a hard time processing what I was seeing. And I hadn't fully processed what I was seeing until . . . And I don't remember where it came from. I think it came from some reporter on TV, who said, "The Capitol has been breached." That was the sentence I heard. And that was the moment when I just was openmouthed because I knew people had amassed in front of the Capitol. They seemed to be trying to get in, it's unclear what's happening. The Capitol has been breached. And then it was just mind-blowing to me. And Julian, you just mentioned the emotion of it. I felt the same way. I felt shocked, and stunned, and angry, and outraged, and openmouthed at what I was seeing. I honestly just couldn't quite believe what I was seeing. And as an historian, I felt I should be thinking grave thoughts or gravitas at this moment. There were no grave thoughts. And I was making no larger connections. It was like a gut punch.

ELIZABETH HINTON: I also had an emotional response initially. I was on Zoom on a call with colleagues and they were getting some information. People were texting them. The texts were popping up on the computer. So at first it was, "Oh, the Capitol has been breached." And then it's, "Oh, there's tear gas at the Capitol. And people are carrying Confederate flags." And that really hit me. Because I was pregnant at the time—beginning of my second semester. And it was just like, "Oh my God. What's going to happen? What does this mean?" And then we ended the meeting, and I calmed down a little bit once I turned on the TV and saw that it was not the worst of what I had imagined it to be.

STEPHANIE MCCURRY: I have a terrible memory and I know I will never forget this. When people talk about "Where were you when Kennedy was shot?" or something . . . I wasn't living in the U.S. then, but I also just don't remember those kinds of things. But I'm pretty sure I will never forget this. I was at home; I was working. And I don't know whether I got an alert on my phone or I checked Twitter, but I was trying to detox from Trump losing and I was on this regime where I wasn't checking the news compulsively. I was very consciously trying to withdraw from being constantly in the daily news cycle. And I knew something was going on in the Capitol that day: the certification of the election. I knew the rally; I knew it could be bad. But I just didn't think of it. And I went in, and I turned the TV on, and I remember it was a moment where the people were scaling the scaffolding that was put up for the inauguration. And I had the exact same reaction as what you guys have been describing, which was I couldn't process. It was complete shock. I kept looking at it, and I kept thinking about Michigan.[1] I could never get that out of my mind anyway. And I kept thinking that this would make sense if it was a state demonstration. But this is the Capitol, and they're in there certifying the election. And that was the part that I just couldn't process: "What does this mean? What's going on?" And I think the scaffolding maybe was around 1:30

[1]   In May 2020, armed mobs stormed the Michigan Capitol in Lansing, protesting the state's authority to impose emergency measures for lockdown during rising mortality rates due to COVID. Between June and September of 2020, fourteen men, many affiliated with right-wing paramilitary organizations, plotted to kidnap Michigan governor Gretchen Whitmer. The men were arrested by the FBI in October of 2020, and several were put on trial and convicted in 2022. "The Co-leader of a Plot to Kidnap Michigan's Governor Gets 16 Years in Prison," NPR, December 27, 2022, https://www.npr.org/2022/12/27/1145632535 /michigan-governor-kidnap-plot-adam-fox-sentencing.

in the afternoon or sometime around then. So there was three more hours of that: of it getting worse and worse.

VARIOUS: [Commentators concurred with McCurry about the time and the happenings.]

MCCURRY: And the sense of helplessness I felt, which I had felt a lot under the Trump years, of "Where's the police?" Those Michigan people were allowed to walk out from the [Capitol] in Michigan, whenever that was. November or whatever. And I thought, "This is crazy. If Black people behaved like this, they would be mowed down in a minute." And there's this constant onrushing of people. More and more people. And then the Trump thing. When he played that video in the afternoon, when they released that video of him, I just remember thinking, "Oh, that was truly traumatic.[2] The helplessness. This isn't just coming from the outside. This is coming from the inside. And he set the fire. And now he's just putting fuel on it. This is evil." That's what it felt like.

JILL LEPORE: So I had the odd experience, that I don't think a lot of people I know had, of having arranged my day around watching the certification live, which is something I've never decided I needed to witness before. But my youngest son was taking a global civics class and he had been really miserable. And his project was about the election and they were studying it. And one thing he had strong views about was the Electoral College. So he had done this part on the Electoral College. And he was

---

2   In a video released the afternoon of January 6, President Trump told protesters who broke into the Capitol that "we had an election that was stolen from us" but "you have to go home now." "President Trump Video Statement on Capitol Protestors," C-SPAN, January 6, 2021, https://www.c-span.org/video/?507774-1 /president-trump-video-statement-capitol-protestors.

remote schooling. And I said, "Look, here's a thing we can do together. Let's go sit down and I'll make—" We had ordered bagels and smoked fish. We were like, "This is going to be great. We're going to watch this. It's going to be unbelievably boring because it's the most routine thing. And it will reassure you that things will be well with our country."

And so we had sat down in this falling apart sectional couch: the kind you sit in and it keeps breaking apart. And you shore up the couch. The chaos of our domestic life. That was going to be remedied by the order and dignity of this quite bureaucratic, boring procedure. So we're sitting there. And then he's like, "There seems like a lot of people outside." We're doing our own little play-by-play: "Jesus, these guys are . . . How come the announcers keep going back to the outside?" Because I want to see what's going on inside. But then the outside . . . We were watching it on CNN, or C-SPAN, or something, flipping around. And there was a real lag. As a viewer, I think, almost, you were more upset than the people who were covering it were, because they had a partial view. Either they were reporting from inside or reporting from one stationary place on the outside. But if you were watching at home, you were getting this Rashomon version of what was going on.[3] And it just seemed much scarier early on.

So we were questioning our own alarm, thinking, "This looks like the end of the country." But they seem to be just reporting the electoral votes being certified. And I think the thing was at 1:30: at the beginning of pulling down the police barricades. At that point, I was like, "Hey, go get your father." And then

3 *Rashomon* is a 1950 Japanese film in which the same set of events is told from different points of view. Thus, the "Rashomon effect" suggests multiple or even contradictory points of view of a specific event.

my other kids were also at home, because it was remote college, wherever. And then by two o'clock, "Go get your brothers." So, by the time they were in, we were all sitting on this decrepit sectional couch that we're always falling off of, just thinking we were watching the Putsch, the Bastille, whatever you want to think that it was.[4] And we just couldn't figure out a way to make sense of it in reference to American history. And I was like, "I am not only the worst parent, but the worst historian." I can't even— [agreement and laughter from Freeman] And I was like, "I know I'm going to get a call any minute to write something about this." And I just want to crawl in bed and put my pillow over my head.

FREEMAN: Right. That I should be able to come up with some smart thing to say immediately because I had written about violence in Congress. It was a very quick enquiry. They were like, "Joanne, you must have something smart to say." And I was still precisely where you were, Stephanie. I was just, "Oh, what just happened?"

WILLIAM STURKEY: I was actually on vacation with my poor fiancée before she left to spend six months in Malawi. And we were trying to spend quality time together. So we had a little house on the beach—even though it was January, it was quite nice—in Carolina Beach. And, of course, my vacation that day involved running a job search, doing a meeting in the afternoon,

4 The Putsch is a reference to what is known as the Munich Putsch or the "Beer Hall Putsch," when, from November 8 to 9, 1923, Adolf Hitler staged what became a failed takeover of the Bavarian government. During the French Revolution, on July 14, 1789, the Bastille, a Parisian royal armory, was stormed by mutinous troops and armed revolutionaries—and thereafter has been a symbol of a populist uprising against a tyrannical government.

and writing an op-ed for the *Washington Post*. God bless her. And then that night, when it finally came time to have dinner and "Let's hang out," I'm just glued to the TV. I was just catching up. And my jaw was just on the floor. Glass of bourbon in my hand. I don't think I touched it. Or maybe I drank the whole thing; I don't know. [Laughter.] Somewhere in between. And I just kept thinking, "This is such a historic moment." Same thing: "Who's going to ask me to write about this?" Or, "How am I going to talk about this?" But really it was just this feeling that I'm going to teach about this for the rest of my life. And I need to bear witness to it now. Even though I knew I didn't understand what was actually happening or what it really meant. But I knew I needed to see it and watch as much as I could to try and understand it. But it did feel quite historic in that moment. It caused a few problems on my vacation. But I'll never forget that moment either.

DOWNS: So can we circle back to some of the themes that a few of you raised? Just as a prequel, Stephanie mentioned Michigan. Could someone talk about Michigan? And the plot to kidnap the governor, Gretchen Whitmer. Was that a trigger for anybody else? Or Stephanie, can you elaborate a little bit more on that? And then I guess the big question, and this is the question behind the entire series, is, "Can history help us in this moment?" Or, "Can historians intervene in some way?" Do we have something to say? Because it seems that we do. But the reaction was, at least in that initial moment, among some, we didn't. And I think it's important for us to state, "Wait a minute. There isn't necessarily an antecedent." Or is there? Or why are we looking for one? Why are we groping toward something that connects us to the past?

MCCURRY: I mean I think there are parts that you can look at and say, "This evokes this." And I'm sure we'll talk about that for the next hour and a half. But I think, partly what I'm hearing from you all, and, I think, myself as I try to process it, is, I don't actually think there is a clear precedent for this. And I also don't think that solutions or directions of response that reiterate the past really work either, because there's not a fit. But the Michigan thing . . . Did anybody else think of that when they were watching it? Because that was an "anti-COVID" protest. That was based on elements of the right-wing response to federal tyranny or state tyranny: overreaching by the government. And I think it was an anti-COVID demonstration, wasn't it? Originally?

HINTON: It was about Governor Whitmer's lockdowns. And when you think about the extent of the anti-COVID protests, or protests alongside the George Floyd racial justice protests, protests against social distancing, and the lockdowns, and mask wearing.[5] By August, those protests had actually surpassed the number for George Floyd. And I remember writing about this in a version of my conclusion for *America on Fire*. Reflecting on those anti-COVID protests made a lot more sense in terms of protesting the act of the election and the "stop the count" protests in many local places. But also, I think many of us were still shocked at the narrow margin and the mobilization of how many people voted for Trump in this election. So I think if we look at these anti-COVID protests, and the extremist and vigilante politics that undergird so many of them, January 6 wasn't

5   The death of George Floyd, a forty-four-year-old Black man who was murdered by a police officer in Minneapolis, kicked off a renewed social justice campaign insisting that Black Lives Matter. These demonstrations across the country and the world erupted in the wake of Floyd's murder on May 25, 2020.

as much of an anomaly. It didn't come out of nowhere in the way that a lot of people describe it.

DOWNS: So would you say . . . Go ahead [directed at Zelizer].

ZELIZER: I was thinking about it. And I felt stunned, upset, and a little discombobulated. But I wasn't surprised. And I literally had spent three hours just talking about the multidecade history of how Republicans had really moved toward the extremes and embraced this vision of partisanship since Gingrich, which I had written this book about [*Burning Down the House: Newt Gingrich, the Fall of a Speaker, and the Rise of the New Republican Party*].⁶ Without guardrails, where you would play to any part of the electorate, you would literally do what was necessary to obtain power. And this had been something I'd talked about. I remember the journalist Barton Gellman wrote a big article in *The Atlantic* before the election on all the ways this election could be subverted. And I had one of the quotes in it.⁷ And I remember a lot of the response was, "Come on. You're being alarmist and this is extreme." [Agreement from McCurry.] "It's not going to happen." But for me, it was very clear that he was serious, Trump, and a lot of Republicans, on potentially mobilizing a challenge to the election. I remember on election night, one of these great Twitter moments for academics. It turned out to be a not-great Twitter moment. But Trump did that press conference. He said, "They're stealing it from me." And I think

6   Newt Gingrich was the fiftieth speaker of the U.S. House of Representatives from 1995 to 1999 and became a conservative author and pundit following his retirement from the House.

7   Barton Gellman, "The Election that Could Break America," *The Atlantic*, November 20, 2020, https://www.theatlantic.com/magazine/archive/2020/11/what-if-trump-refuses-concede/616424/.

I tweeted out, "This is one of the worst moments in American history." And of course, everyone began piling on me: "Come on. What about . . . ?" Naming every other bad moment.

DOWNS: I remember that.

ZELIZER: Yeah. Even our son came the next day and said his friends were talking about it.

FREEMAN: But I was going to say: the thing about that, Julian, is that that's the truest testament to your feeling at that moment. And that's the real value of it. That's precisely what it felt like. Even if we all, as historians, would do exactly what Twitter did to you.

ZELIZER: Right. But it was at the moment you could see what he was doing and where this was going. In some ways, it was actually worse than I imagined. He was setting up a really threatening challenge, from the position of the presidency, to the integrity of the election. He was doing this in plain sight. He was appealing to these same groups who had been part of his coalition for the last four years. And so when it unfolded, part of my response was that that's where this was going all along. And it's that threatening, what the administration and a lot of Republicans were doing. And it made total sense. That night, I thought of Michigan, actually. Now they were going to the Capitol, armed and loaded and ready to go. For me, there are two different ways for the historian to approach a moment like this: There is the popular historical question of "What's the comparison? Did this happen before? What is this like?" But there's the other kind of question, the one that interests me more, about the long-term framework for understanding where something like January 6 came from: How do we understand why these people stormed the Capitol, threatened members of

Congress, in a broader historical trajectory? And I think there is a way to see the history, certainly, of contemporary politics, and it makes sense rather than perceiving this to be a total aberration.

LEPORE: I really appreciate the way you divide those into two different piles: "What are the precedents for this?" and "What is the long-term story?" Because I think the first question is really an impoverished one, and it really impoverishes our political discourse. And I believe that that's where historians are most often called upon, is to offer up some kind of fake analogy: "This is just like . . ." So I remember the next day there were all these people talking about the Puerto Rican nationalists in 1954.[8] And I was like, "What the fuck?" [Laughter.] "This is a completely different animal." This is really just a cable news tic: Yank some historian onto the stage. "Tell me some sure things you know about that we don't know about, that, 'This is a little bit like . . .' And then go away. We never want to hear from you again." I feel like that's an exhausting move. And I think, with regard to the entire rise of Trump and his administration, it really diminished the quality of historians' engagement with the problem of Trumpism. Because, I don't know about you guys, but I feel like I was really called on much more than even ever before to [answer] "Who is he like? Is he like Huey Long plus George Wallace? If you add a little bit of . . . Andrew Jackson . . . 20 percent George Wallace . . ."[9] And I just felt there was a point at

8   In March 1954, four Puerto Rican nationalists opened fire from the public galleries of the U.S. House of Representatives. Five members of Congress were injured.

9   Huey Long (1893–1935) was the governor of Louisiana from 1928 to 1932, then served as one of the state's U.S. senators until he was assassinated in 1935. To combat the Depression, he advocated a transfer of wealth from rich to poor and increased government spending. George Wallace (1919–98) served four nonconsecutive terms as governor of Alabama. He is best known for blocking

which . . . There was one day I woke up and it was not January 6 of 2021. It was sometime in 2015, when I was like, "This is entirely without precedent. This is a new day in American history." And you can ask a historian to talk about its novelty and Julian does that so well. But it was an act of weird, strange, contorted containment to try to make it be like it was something that happened before.

FREEMAN: But I totally agree with what you're saying. [Referring to Lepore.] But I also think the impulse behind that, in part was, "Make us feel better."

LEPORE: Yeah.

FREEMAN: "By finding something in the past that you can connect this to." So I agree.

LEPORE: But we should not feel better!

FREEMAN: No!

So I was constantly being asked, "Well, Joanne, it's been worse, right?"

LEPORE: Hey, it's true. And it's okay.

FREEMAN: Precisely. It was like, "Okay, you can't make that kind of comparison." As you just said, Julian, in a sense, we weren't surprised that it happened, but we were shocked to see it. And we can see that there are historical roots to it. But there is not an exact precedent in American history. And anyone looking to history to feel better about this moment is just not looking at this moment. They're just trying to put a mask of the past over it. And really, to look ahead in time, and to look at the legacy of what's going on, and the impact of what's going on, you need

---

the desegregation of the University of Alabama in June 1963 and for declaring in his first inaugural address: "Segregation now, segregation tomorrow, segregation forever."

to look at the weird conglomeration of things that are coming together right now, that are acting on that stake right now. So just as you said, Jill, if you're looking to find the five things that are most like this moment, that does precisely nothing.

MCCURRY: But I think that the long-term run up to this is not confusing. I think from the Klan forward.[10] From the very moment of emancipation, the first test of democracy and emancipation, there was this murderous connection of democracy and white supremacy. It was just this backlash from then on. And that domestic terrorism movement has never properly been recognized for what it was. We hardly even teach it anymore, the first Klan. There's not very much known about that. And so that right-wing, incredibly empowered, paramilitary, reactionary form of politics of the United States, the violent politics, doesn't surprise me at all. And I just think that that's a really long history that nobody wants to own.

DOWNS: Right.

MCCURRY: But what shocked me about it was, it's at the Capitol. So it's both things. It's not surprising. And also, one other thing I want to say about that, I just cannot get my mind around the sense of empowerment these people feel. They feel Teflon. They aren't going to be even maced for behaving like this. And that sense of legitimacy, it's connected to this business about the election being illegitimate. It's "Who are the people?" Well, "We are

10 Founded in 1865, the Ku Klux Klan (kkk) was a white supremacist "fraternal" organization and a vehicle for white southern resistance to the Republican Party's efforts to establish political equality for Black people after the Civil War. Former Confederate general Nathan Bedford Forrest was the first leader of the Klan, called "an Invisible Empire of the South." See Alan Trelease, *White Terror: The Ku Klux Klan Conspiracy and Southern Reconstruction*, 2nd ed. (New York: Praeger, 1979).

the people. They are not." And that's the fundamental question all the way through American history, with very violent denunciations of anybody outside that original circle saying, "Well, we're the people too." So it's really frightening. And the fact that they could turn on the Capitol with the authorization of the President, on the day of the so-called peaceful transfer of power. Okay, yeah, I know who those people are. I know why they're there. That's what the Confederate flag is doing. It's signaling what they're doing. But it's still new. It's still new.

STURKEY: I think you're onto something. And it is a little tricky when they ask us to compare events: "What is the one event from the past that this event looked just like?" But to me, it's more about trends. And I think there are trends. To me, it very closely mirrors the overthrow of Reconstruction in the South: 1875, Mississippi, First Mississippi Plan;[11] 1898, Wilmington, North Carolina. Armed militia, white militia, in the streets trying to overthrow an election. And very successfully doing so. And the thing that I think is really ominous is that we're not in a moment where we've seen the end of it. I think in 2012, had I said, "Okay, a southern governor is going to openly call for people with guns to go to a polling place," that might shock a lot of people. If I said that in 2024, I think that could quite possibly happen. And I think, to me, that's what it really reminded me of, was those two moments: Wilmington, 1898, or Mississippi, 1875. And that's exactly right: we haven't taught these at all. *Wilmington's Lie* just won the Pulitzer a year ago.[12] Many people

---

11 The Mississippi Plan used intimidation and fraud to ensure that white Democratic candidates would win elections in the post–Civil War era.

12 David Zucchino, *Wilmington's Lie: The Murderous Coup of 1898 and the Rise of White Supremacy* (New York: Grove Atlantic, 2020).

in my state [North Carolina] have no idea what happened in Wilmington, 1898, even if they're from there. And I think that's a real failure of American history not to teach that. But I think that's quite frightening. But that's what it reminded me of. And the other thing is that there are literally moments in local newspapers and from those white militia readers that, if you pulled those quotes and said somebody on January 6 said them . . .

MCCURRY: Yeah.

STURKEY: . . . a lot of those people would believe you. Not, "Hey, let's go out and shoot Black people," but, sayings along the lines of "We must take back our governments, the white man's government. White men must rule." Those sorts of things. If you heard a reporter say that somebody in the crowd of January 6 said those things, I think we would all buy it. And that comes directly from the coverage of those events in the 1890s, 1870s.

DOWNS: Joanne, I was wondering if you could jump in on this? Because at the end of your second book . . . And I can't remember the title and I can't Google it. I want to say *The Affairs of Bloody Violence*?

VARIOUS: [Crosstalk and laughter]

MCCURRY: *The Field of Blood: Violence in Congress and the Road to the Civil War.*[13]

DOWNS: Yes. You have this fascinating argument where you assert there's violence in Congress—and this goes to Stephanie's point and to Will's point—but then as soon as Reconstruction happens, violence goes to the South. It develops into the Klan.

---

13 Joanne Freeman, *The Field of Blood: Violence in Congress and the Road to the Civil War* (New York: Picador, 2019).

That was such an original, fascinating intervention. And I was wondering if you could just elaborate on that.

FREEMAN: Well, connecting to what Stephanie said about this long tradition of violence being used by white supremacists, the book is about, for the most part, southerners using violence, and threats, and intimidation to get what they want. So bullying their way into getting what they want, which obviously has a very long tradition.

DOWNS: Fascinating. But also to go back to Jill's question too: "When does this impulse for historians to weigh in on a particular moment develop?" Is it coming from historians trying to push themselves onto the public stage and say, "This current event reminds me of X"? Or is it journalists who suggest, "We need to have historical perspective"? I know historians have been public intellectuals for a very long time—before Julian, before Jill, there have been others. But, "Was that a popular rhetorical practice for those earlier generations of historians to frame contemporary events?" This is the premise behind the vertical Made by History at the *Washington Post*.[14] It takes current events and says, "Let's find the antecedent." But I'm wondering if we can think of when this actually started to happen.

LEPORE: So I have a theory about that, but it's out of my hat. We compare it to investigative evidence. It's the same argument that you're making. It isn't about collapsing the distance between now and 1898; it's about pointing out continuities. You were saying you can make a sustained explanation. This is the other thing that Julian was suggesting. And that's how we ordinarily work. That's how we teach. That's how we write. But there's a

14 A column introduced by the *Washington Post* in 2017.

certain time of being called into the public square when you know you're going to be asked. And you're like, "Isn't this just like that? Okay. 2020, 1968." Elizabeth, explain. [Laughter.] You might have five minutes. And then, goodbye.

DOWNS: Right.

HINTON: Yeah. Right.

LEPORE: And that's not a historical analysis that's going to help illuminate the relation between Reconstruction and the rejection of Reconstruction in this moment. I think if I were to guess . . .

DOWNS: Go.

LEPORE: . . . where it comes from, I think that Vietnam and Watergate were a kind of reset, where people were like, "These things are new." Okay. This is new. So everything else since then, every other intervention—"Is this another Vietnam?" That's how journalistic discourse took place.

DOWNS: Right.

LEPORE: Every presidential misdeed: "Is this another Watergate?" Everything's a "gate." So I think that that was a new era in journalism. That rise of adversarial newspaper journalism that we associate the [*Washington*] *Post* with. And I think it became a journalistic form that maybe is unnamed. But it's the "then-now, now-as-then move." It's like an accordion that they want to go [Lepore makes the sound of an accordion]. And then that's the only noise that historians are allowed to make. But we have a symphony of instruments behind us. And this is the only thing we're allowed to say. So we think about the failure of historical interpretation that makes what the hell happened on that day legible, that we, who even do this work, are struggling to come up with. What's the public supposed to make of it? When all they really get are these weird, little bleeps of . . . Elizabeth, did you not feel that way about being asked about various protests and stuff?

HINTON: Yes, I think for the most part. Although there are moments when I feel—and this might not be in the mainstream news . . . But you can have really engaged conversations with people who are asking me to provide that long-term analysis and talk about continuities and not just 1968, 2021. Let's do it. Protests. And think more deeply about what are the social forces and the conditions that lead people to resist? Or let's think about the longer history of police brutality, and mob violence and where that comes from, and white mob violence. It's something that, I agree, Stephanie, we don't talk about enough. Which is why, when the sixth happens, it's difficult to understand or see where it comes from.

MCCURRY: Where do you start? Even if they ask you to explain that, the then and the now, which "then"? Where are you going to start? You can say, "Okay, here's two events." But I also think that, or I wonder that, maybe Jill is pointing towards this, but we're only invited . . . As you said, for the most part, you get two minutes and then you're gone. And so is it possible to say that maybe we've adapted too much to this? For example, the Made by History [column] in the *Washington Post*: sometimes I just get really frustrated when I read those things, because it's the most immediate cut-and-paste thing. [Agreement from several commentators.] And they're soliciting them all the time. But on the other hand—and I don't know if this is what you had in mind, Elizabeth, but—sometimes when I read people like [*New York Times* Opinion writer] Jamelle Bouie, I'm just so impressed at the way he can distill a bunch of serious scholarship and extract its contemporary relevance. We don't just make our contributions by getting two minutes in Made by History or on TV. You make it by publishing your books, which some journalists read. It seems to me that's one really healthy thing. And I don't know if you guys think that that has always been true. But I think in this crisis of Trump and after, the level of journalistic engagement with historians seems to me just so incredibly rewarding. It's not me. It's just us. And I can read [Bouie's] column or Jelani Cobb . . . Well Jelani Cobb is a historian.[15] But there's a lot of journalism with real historical depth. And they're citing their sources. They're citing their historians—particularly Jamelle Bouie. Do you think it's only him though?

ZELIZER: Well . . . before Trump . . .

LEPORE: So, I remember—I'm talking too much, but one thing: When I was watching on the sixth, I remembered a trip that I took in 2009 to D.C. to be on a panel about the Tea Party. And Dick Armey and Tucker Carlson were the other panelists.[16]

HINTON: Oh, wow.

LEPORE: And Dick Armey had arranged to have all the tickets sold in advance—they were free but you had to register—to

---

15 Jelani Cobb earned a PhD from Rutgers in 2003 in history and has been a staff writer for the *New Yorker* since 2015 and dean of the Columbia School of Journalism since 2022.

16 The Tea Party was a conservative movement in the early twenty-first century that preached fiscal and political conservatism. In 2009, members of this Congressional caucus supported small government and opposed universal health care. In 2016, the Tea Party as a separate political force was welcomed into the right-tilting Republican fold. Dick Armey of Texas served in the House of Representatives from 1985 to 2003 and was a staunch Tea Party supporter. Tucker Carlson was a talk show host on the Fox News Network from 2016 to 2023. Also see, Jill Lepore, *The White of Their Eyes: The Tea Party's Revolution and the Battle over American History* (Princeton: Princeton University Press, 2011).

people from Freedom Works.[17] So when I got there, the entire room was full of people with the Freedom Works T-shirts and hats, which were the MAGA hat of the Tea Party. And it was on September 11. It was the day that they'd all come down to D.C. from all over the country for the Glenn Beck 9/12 rally, which is the thing—[18]

MCCURRY: How did you get pulled into this?

LEPORE: Kate Zernike from the *New York Times* was the other person on the panel.[19] Well, I'll just tell the story because this is just too good. In the green room, Armey and Carlson had this elaborate conversation about hunting in Africa and the different endangered species that they'd killed. And I was just sitting there thinking, "How much of an idiot do you think I am?" Obviously you didn't go kill an endangered species. It was just this stupid liberal baiting thing. And I was like, "These are not going to be tough people to argue with." [Laughter.] They were just so unimpressive. Anyway, afterward . . . So I don't have to talk about the event, but it was very illuminating what the people in the audience thought the American Revolution and the Civil War were about, which came out in the discussion. But afterward, a lot of people came up to talk to me. And I remember I had this Texas couple. So everybody was white evangelicals from Texas. And I was trying to have a friendly chat with them. And

17 Freedom Works remains a right-wing and libertarian advocacy group.
18 Glenn Beck is a right-wing pundit and founder of the Tea Party. He organized a series of September 12 rallies across the United States in 2009 to reignite the American spirit of "patriotism and resolve" (as September 12 was the day after September 11, 2001—the most dramatic terrorist attack in American history).
19 Zernike is Pulitzer Prize–winning *New York Times* national correspondent. See also Kate Zernike, *Boiling Mad: Inside Tea Party America* (New York: St. Martin's Press, 2011).

I was like, "Wow, it's such a beautiful September weekend to be in D.C. What else are you doing while you're here? The rally, I know you're doing that." [Laughter.] "But have you been to the monuments? What about the National Portrait Gallery? You could go to the Presidential Hall. What are you going to see? Have you thought about going over to the Arlington National?" Just trying to think about things they would enjoy. And their faces dropped. And they said, "This is a city built in honor of the federal government and we don't believe in the federal government. We hate every block and street corner of the nation's capital." And I was like, "Okay. I don't think I can stay in this conversation." But I thought about that watching the Capitol stuff. The Capitol is, to them, a monument that it doesn't appear to be to me, in a way that has taken a really long time to persuade them of. I don't think you'd get Texans fifty years ago saying that they hate Washington, D.C., in the same way. Maybe I'm wrong. But I don't know where I was going with that story. But yeah.

DOWNS: Julian, maybe you can answer. How does that tie into your book on Gingrich and the changes in the Republican Party?[20] Does that become part of the ideology of Republicans?

ZELIZER: Okay. So not the media's question. You mean—

DOWNS: Just the example that Jill gave of these people. Where does this sentiment come from?

ZELIZER: So you can take many points, certainly from the seventies, and you can go back even further, where you can see elements of the party changing. So you could take a Newt Gingrich, who spent a lot of the 1980s arguing that Republicans

20 Julian Zelizer, *Burning Down the House: Newt Gingrich, the Fall of a Speaker, and the Rise of the New Republican Party* (New York: Penguin Press, 2020).

needed to eliminate the boundaries and guardrails that they, the older generation of Republicans, still adhered to. He argued that Republicans needed to be much more aggressive because it would be impossible to amass power if they were not willing to essentially do anything to take down the Democrats. And "do anything" for Gingrich in the eighties might not be what it is to Trump—he was even more extreme—but it was that same basic philosophy: You start to manipulate basic processes of government, for example, to achieve power, or inject toxic rhetoric into the public square on a normal basis. You're willing to bring down opponents in pretty vicious ways and spread disinformation. And part of what that Republican Party did—and Lee Atwater is another example of a figure who saw this nexus—was to connect the party to extremist groups who are taking the antigovernment philosophy of Reagan and putting it on steroids essentially.[21] And so, I think, in addition to Michigan, another historical memory that came to mind of January 6 was the tragic Oklahoma City bombing. There was a moment in 1995 where this horrendous act of white domestic extremism was front and center, as the guilty parties showed the willingness to use violence and murder. McVeigh and Nichols were connected to a broadening of these organizations in the United States during that period.[22]

21 Lee Atwater (1951–1991) was a political consultant for the Republican Party who was famous for his scurrilous tactics.

22 On April 19, 1995—two years to the day after the Waco Siege and mass deaths of seventy-six Branch Davidians, followers of David Koresh—antigovernment white nationalist extremists Terry Nichols and Timothy McVeigh blew up a federal building in Oklahoma City, killing 168 people and injuring another 800.

And one of the arguments about Oklahoma City is that the act of terrorism was emblematic, in the mid-nineties already, of how far portions of the public had moved toward seeing the government literally as the enemy. And so the party, especially from the Tea Party to the Trump years, became more comfortable as part of a new strategy of stoking these elements. Of course, the antigovernment philosophy has been around for a while. Certainly since Ronald Reagan. The ideas swirling around the insurrection are just a very extreme version of it. We've seen it was simply brought into mainstream Republican politics. So I don't know. I was just thinking of what Jill said. When tackling moments like these, I definitely prefer to answer the long-term trajectory question ["What events in history can January 6 be traced to?"] rather than the "What is this like?" question. I think [media outlets] sometimes get frustrated with me. Occasionally I'll make a comparison, but usually I'm the guy who doesn't give you that kind answer. They prefer that answer. And I think it's a bit—

LEPORE: Why do you think that is?

ZELIZER: I think for some reporters it's about time. They don't even have two minutes for a discussion. It's more like thirty seconds. The comparison is something quick they can get from a historian that won't mean we're talking for ten minutes. "What's this like?" I think Joanne's right. It is also a comfort. You see January 6, and I think many people just want to say, we've had something like this before.

MCCURRY: And we survived it.

ZELIZER: Right.

MCCURRY: [Like] the Civil War, which, in fact, contrary to popular belief, we actually survived.

ZELIZER: I think there is also a history that sometimes reporters, and the public, don't want. You could go deep in the history in ways that are profoundly uncomfortable. You could talk about the white backlash politics of the past few years and say, "Oh, yeah, this actually makes sense. Look at the South during the Jim Crow era. And look at white supremacist ideology and organizations since whatever period." Meaning, it is even worse than you think. Some of this is as American as apple pie. I try to give them that kind of answer as well, probably to my detriment. Because I think that is where the history usually takes you on some of these questions.

FREEMAN: I want to qualify this because my impression is that, despite the people sitting in this room, there actually aren't that many historians who are necessarily being called to testify. Some of them are being interviewed . . .

ZELIZER: Yeah.

FREEMAN: And their material used. But if you watch cable news, it's very rarely a historian who's asked to say something.

ZELIZER: Right.

FREEMAN: And there's all these historians.

LEPORE: There's a go-to list of the people that will deliver that very wisely.

FREEMAN: Precisely. There's a handful. And then there's all these historians gnashing their teeth that are like, "Oh, come on. There's so much that . . ." And part of the problem, I think, is what you're pointing to, Julian, is correct, which is what we want to say is not [what journalists want]. "This reminds me of 1870. Bing, and goodbye, and thank you, and good night." We don't want to do that. And maybe some people are more willing to do that. But I think there would be better ways of making use of historians that could do some of the things that we're talking about here to at least get people thinking outside of the realm of the tracks that they run on. I do a lot of public-minded history work that isn't necessarily TV, but podcasts and webcasts. And part of the reason I put the energy into that is because it feels to me people fundamentally don't understand a lot of really basic things and aren't going to listen to it coming to them as a lesson. But if you put the information out there in an inviting voice, some people actually might hear it. So, as a historian, at this moment—because you've mentioned a few times, Jim—it is about the public.

DOWNS: Right.

FREEMAN: I feel like it's vitally important for some of us to be figuring out the best way to address the public, to inform them about democracy and how it works.

DOWNS: Right.

FREEMAN: One of the reasons why I'm on Twitter as much as I am is that, very early on, I referenced something about checks and balances, and a lot of people didn't know what that meant. And I said, "Oh, okay, well, let me explain what it is." And then I got all these people responding saying, "Oh, I always wondered what checks and balances meant."[23] Okay, well, we need to be filling that space.

DOWNS: Yep.

ZELIZER: The problem with January 6, if we see it as this isolated moment, you don't see just how systematic all the different

---

23 "Checks and balances" refers to the separation of powers that results from divided branches of government outlined in the U.S. Constitution, which is intended to divide power among the three branches of government—executive, legislative, and judicial—to prevent any single entity from having too much power. This principle was outlined by Montesquieu in his 1748 treatise De l'Esprit des Loix.

efforts were to undercut the election. To be sure, it wasn't inevitable that we would end up with people storming the Capitol and some willing to threaten the lives of elected officials. But there was a logic to it, and the problem didn't go away after January 6. This whole year of manipulating the electoral process, along with the ongoing attacks on voting rights, points to antidemocratic forces on the right. That had been going on for a while. And I worry that when we either don't look at how this campaign unfolded and where it came from or when we treat this as a comparison by saying, "Hey, people fought in Congress, and isn't this just a new version of it?" we end up with a real lack of understanding about its roots and where this might be going. Right now . . . I don't know how true this is, but there are articles emerging about former President Trump intervening in Senate races around the country . . .

DOWNS: Right.

ZELIZER: . . . which means the story continues. This is where the lack of historical discussion can be damaging. Because you see it almost as this bizarre, ugly one-off as opposed to part of a much broader, systematic effort.

LEPORE: So I used to think that, really, historians were to blame for this. And I do think that to some degree.

FREEMAN: To blame for what?

LEPORE: For the cripplingly limited notion of historical change over time that the American public has. And I will blame it on the retreat from the academy that was the aftermath of Vietnam. But now I wonder . . . I was trained to never participate in any public exchange about anything as a historian. And there are reasons for that. But they largely all come down to Vietnam. But then someone said to me once at a public event, "Well, environmental scientists have been doing their best job in public sphere and trying to explain climate science." And now we could say public health practitioners and infectious disease specialists are doing their best job in the public sphere trying to explain pandemics and virology. So it isn't maybe enough to find a way to have eight thousand words instead of four hundred, or ten minutes instead of thirty seconds. I'm not sure whether if more of us did things or did different things, that it would make a difference. That's my—

MCCURRY: I don't think historians have that power. I fundamentally disagree with you about that.

LEPORE: Okay. Yes.

MCCURRY: I just really don't. I think that's a misplaced assessment of a world of politics and knowledge that we just are small players. And in this country, especially. And there are other countries in the world where intellectuals have a bigger place and voice routinely in public life. And it's not an accident that we don't. I don't think it's just a matter of—

LEPORE: It's not our fault that we don't?

ZELIZER: I have a question about that.

MCCURRY: Our fault? No. We live in a commercialized media landscape and a world of institutional power. That universities themselves are the only place where we can make a living doing what we do, by definition, marginalizes us from the rough and tumble of that public . . . I think what we do is important. I also don't think . . . I'm not sure whether we're talking about January 6 or the world of historians and the media.

DOWNS: The discussion is supposed to cover this ground—about how historians respond to the headlines. That's the point of this series. This conversation is good. It's very good. This is amazing. It's important that you're talking about these things.

FREEMAN: But related to what you just said, Stephanie, and what you said as well, Jill, you spoke as though it was a long time ago that the academy was saying you should never do anything for the public. The fact of the matter is the academy doesn't appreciate it now. They don't let you do any of that kind of stuff. Anything that an academic does to speak to the public and engage with the public, you do that either for yourself and for the public—or even to the detriment of what a university thinks about you.

LEPORE: Well, I think that's true. But to Stephanie's point, it wouldn't make any difference if we did or didn't.

MCCURRY: I think you're [Lepore] trying to shoulder your way into a media landscape, and a media power game, and also a political power game that we're just not players in. We're intellectuals. And that's why I think the contribution we make is actually the raw materials of other things.

LEPORE: Mm-hmm.

MCCURRY: At least that's certainly how I think about it, in part. It's not that we shouldn't try. I don't disagree with you about that, Jill, and I appreciate all the things that you do, and Joanne does, and that Julian does. All of these things matter. But I don't think you can turn around and say that we have a fucked-up view of American history because historians haven't done enough. I think there's a lot of reasons. Some of them involved with the Republican Party and the capture of the Republican Party by extremist elements, which was not entirely predictable, but, at a certain point, became so. But I also think that it is itself an expression of political economy and power and race and gender power in our society. It isn't separate from those things. And if we try . . . I think it would be actually quite impossible to put yourself at the center of this discussion. And I'm not sure that's the most important thing anyway. I think it's just that we are in the play of power. And you can't individually just sort of bootstrap yourself into a different position, structurally, in the society, and in either political economy or in a world of knowledge. The places where knowledge is produced. It's clear from what we're discussing, and the January 6 insurrection itself, and Julian's account of the way Republican politics works now, or what you just said about the pandemic is it's not information that's lacking. Because the information itself is a tool in the political struggle. So I just don't think that this is about what we do, and whether we do it right, and whether we do enough of it.

DOWNS: I want to get Will in on that.

STURKEY: I'm going to make two disparate points and a question. So, to answer your question, I think a lot of it has to do with the good-meaning centrist folks realizing that America isn't what they thought it was. And they're like, "Oh my God. How can this possibly be?" And then we turn to historians. I think it has something to do with that too. With Julian's point, I thought that was interesting about the federal government. That's always been there, certainly. But I think it basically had an injection of steroids when Obama was elected president. And I think we make a little bit too much of Obama as a central figure. It's actually, I think, more about the people who loved Obama. It's not necessarily Obama walking out on the stage at Grand Park. It's the people in the crowd wearing the T-shirts, the Black voters who helped elect him into office. That's when the antigovernment appeal expands toward everyday, normal people who aren't the nut jobs that want to go bomb buildings. And I think the point about Vietnam is interesting too. Yes, there's people who lost their careers over Vietnam, certainly. But it also occurs to me that that is the moment when the public faith in the academy begins to diminish. But it's also the moment when the academy changes a lot. We get women's studies, Black studies. The academy becomes way more diverse. And also academic departments and academics are supporting the civil rights movement. So I'm not just sure it's just Vietnam, although the point is well taken. We know historians who lost their careers for that.

ZELIZER: Right. Because that's the point that I was thinking about that brings Jill's comment and Stephanie's comment together. Which is that there are questions about how historians deliver their information. And yet there are serious cultural, huge, explosive debates that are predicated on history, namely the 1619 Project. So it's a historical argument that came from a journalist, Nikole Hannah-Jones.[24] There are many people who think about the American Revolution. So many books have been written about slavery as well. Nikole Hannah-Jones figured out a way to frame 1619 as a way to call into question 1776 and our national origin story. And that's a journalist's way of delivering historical analysis, which was much more efficacious than what a lot of historians can do. So, to me, it seems—can we think about the delivery of historical analysis? Nikole Hannah-Jones would argue that she is building on this information that historians have done. But there is a point where she's framed it. And

24 Hannah-Jones joined the *New York Times* as a staff writer in 2015 and won a MacArthur Fellowship in 2017. In 2020, she was awarded a Pulitzer Prize for her work on the 1619 Project.

that's a root, in part, of January 6. Because I kept on thinking when I saw January 6 that they are fighting against this understanding of our past. And this is what Elizabeth, I think, was getting at too. There were obviously many impulses. They're fighting against the lockdowns. They're fighting against their history wars and the 1619 Project, in part, too. Not that that's a motivation in their minds: "I'm against Nikole Hannah-Jones." But they're against the recentering of a narrative that doesn't keep 1776 front and center.

MCCURRY: Well, that doesn't keep white people at the center. It's not 1619. The 1619 Project is the displacement of white people.

HINTON: Right. There are three groups that dissipated. There are the Trump supporters and the QAnon people.[25] But the extremist violent people at the frontlines were really committed to calls to white supremacy and replacement theory—the idea that when people of color and women have rights that somehow takes away or infringes on the rights of white people and white men in particular. I think Barack Obama, especially, was this national symbol of that process in the context of massive demographic changes. And so the 1619 Project, and the work that so many of us do to reckon with the history of oppression and exploitation in this country, directly runs up against that worldview and the kind of society that those who participated in the sixth were trying to bring to fruition. I think historian Kathleen Belew talked about this a lot in her book [*Bring the*

25 In October 2017, an anonymous user put a series of posts on the internet message board 4chan. This user signed off as "Q," and within a few years, QAnon has become a source of political conspiracy theories and disruptive disinformation. Experts have labeled this movement "a digital cult." Followers of QAnon were deeply involved in the January 6 event at the U.S. capitol.

War Home: The White Power Movement and Paramilitary America (Harvard University Press, 2019)]. That moment was really a recruitment event to get these other factions within the right on board in this larger politics of extremism. This is where, I think, historical insight can be really important . . . in demographic change and in the aftermath of war.

DOWNS: Right.

HINTON: Belew talks about this too: That the most important factor in terms of recruitment for the far right and white supremacists is after war. After the Civil War, after World War I, after the Vietnam War. And now, I think, we can really think about the Gulf War, which also played into the Oklahoma City bombing, and the War on Terror, as laying the new foundations for the Gen Xers and the millennials that we really saw rise up on January 6.

MCCURRY: I was thinking a lot about Kathleen Belew's work, when I was reading Jim's questions, because of "the bring the war home" argument. And then we watched this January 6 insurrection, and these paramilitary . . . Oath Keepers and people who arrived in tactical gear, who were the tip of the spear.[26] And the second one in the line is this woman who was an army veteran.

---

26 The Oath Keepers (formed in 2009) are self-styled "Guardians of the Republic" who have recruited members from the military and law enforcement, among others the Oath Keepers have been organizing "militias" since 2013. They promote conspiracy theories and were present at the Unite the Right rallies in Charlottesville, Virginia in 2017. Seventeen members of the group have been charged for crimes associated with their role in events in Washington, D.C., on January 6. Founded in 2016, the Proud Boys (militant misogynists and anti-Semites) were present as well at Charlottesville and served as an "invading force" on January 6. The leader of the group and several comrades were put on trial for "seditious conspiracy," a plot to keep Trump in the White House despite Biden's 2020 election.

Ashli Babbitt was an air force veteran.[27] So we change our military. There's always been this danger that it's the military . . . Probably has to do with the desegregation of the military as being more in advance of the larger social process.[28] So the reaction is more intense and comes there first. And now we're seeing women radicalized as former members of the armed services. And it's not that it's not surprising. It's not that; we're surprised to see women in these right-wing groups. It comes from both strands, as you said: the more generic Republican extremism of dispossession. "We used to be the center of the story. Our rights were our privileges. Who are these people? They're illegitimate." This instinctive sense of loss that turns really ugly. So there's tons of women. You saw them out there: Women for Trump or Women for America First. And they have their banners. And those organizations we've known for a long time. But then these women in tactical gear pushing . . . There's something more than five or eight of them have been indicted already, and numbers of them are former armed forces members. So that's a measure of what has changed in, what, the last thirty years? When did you start to see serious numbers of women in the armed forces? In combat positions?

27 Ashli Babbitt was a military veteran and QAnon supporter who was shot and killed by a Capitol guard on January 6. She died with a Trump flag wrapped around her neck, while she was being hoisted over a barrier during the breach of the U.S. Capitol. Lois Beckett and Vivian Ho, "'She Was Deep into It': Ashli Babbitt, Killed in Capitol Riot, Was Devoted Conspiracy Theorist," *The Guardian*, January 9, 2021.

28 Only recently has historical scholarship emphasized that the U.S. military was the first major institution to officially desegregate, following President Harry S. Truman's Executive Order 9981 issued in July 1948. See, for example, Rawn James Jr., *The Double V: How Wars, Protest, and Harry Truman Desegregated America's Military* (New York: Bloomsburg, 2013).

FREEMAN: But this is another way in which framing matters.

DOWNS: Exactly.

FREEMAN: And this gets back to 1619 and 1776. Because, among the many reasons why this particular population prefer 1776, the whites are at the center of the story. It's all capital letters, "The Revolution." And that is claimed by these people. They are revolutionaries, and they're fighting tyranny. And they are founders. They claim that mantle for themselves. It's the word "revolution" and the idea of revolution. And we saw that on January 6. There was someone dressed as George Washington, kneeling with a flag or something. There's this famous painting of Washington kneeling in the snow, praying for the Revolution. Someone acted that out on the steps of the Capitol. So there's this claiming of the Revolution as theirs, which, to them, sanctifies what they're doing and makes it the most ultimately American thing that it could possibly be. And anyone who's opposed to them becomes, by definition with that, the bad guy. And that relies on a nonunderstanding of the revolution . . .

DOWNS: Right, right.

FREEMAN: . . . and the most simplified version of it. So that's central.

STURKEY: Just real quick: That makes me think of those Jon McNaughton paintings, where he's literally painting Trump with George Washington, and Abraham Lincoln, and all these other people.[29]

[Laughter.]

29 See Daniel Lippmann, "He Rose to Fame Painting Trump Realism," Politico, April 21, 2022, https://www.politico.com/news/2022/04/21/trump-painter -00026676.

LEPORE: And I interviewed people for the Tea Party book that I wrote called *The Whites of Their Eyes*,[30] which was really making the claim that it was really important to these people to imagine a revolution that never happened. And that was the particular comic book version of American history that they were taught in school, in fairness to them. And then it had become urgently important to them during the bicentennial.[31] Mostly older [people]. And they felt they got cheated out of this patriotic bicentennial that they desperately wanted, as a generation, to recover from Vietnam. And instead there was the People's Bicentennial Commission that Howard Zinn was on.[32] And there was the whole protest of the bicentennial by people on the left instead of the Nixon Commission that they wanted to go forward and to be able to celebrate with. And they would talk about that. They remembered the protests in Boston, over the Boston Tea Party anniversary.[33] And I think, for me, that's really powerful and illuminating, because I'm a historian, and so people's

---

30 Jill Lepore, *The Whites of their Eyes: The Tea Party's Revolution and the Battle over American History* (Princeton: Princeton University Press, 2010).

31 Celebrated on July 4, 1976, the U.S. Bicentennial marked the two hundredth anniversary of the signing of the Declaration of Independence. There were many events, observations, and groups that were created in response to this national milestone.

32 Howard Zinn (1922–2010) was an American activist and historian whose 1980 *A People's History of the United States* became a best seller and appeared in popular media like *The Sopranos, The Simpsons,* and *Good Will Hunting.*

33 A 1973 reenactment sponsored by the city of Boston to mark the two hundredth anniversary of the Boston Tea Party became the scene of protests calling for environmental protection, racial justice, an end to corporate profiteering, and the impeachment of Richard Nixon. See "Protest and Commemoration at the 1973 Boston Tea Party Anniversary," YouTube, https://www.youtube.com /watch?v=7nwG1HfRje8.

fascination with history seems to carry a lot of explanatory force for me, but on the other hand, it was just a marker for them about their decline. They're not really that interested in history. They're just really not. They're not really interested in the 1619 Project. They're just not. The people carrying the "Don't Tread on Me" flags—it's cosplay.[34] We live in an age of superheroes and Halloween costumes. It's not nothing, but it's not what we think about when we're talking about history. It's a marker of their decline.

I'm trying to picture someone new. Not someone who was involved in the insurrection, but people who voted for Trump who feel like the country's falling apart and Trump was going to save them. And they didn't really like him but they voted for him anyway. They would hear us: "What are you even talking about? I'm suffering out here. Progressives have failed to relieve my suffering. I sat through Clinton and Obama and I didn't get what I need. And you, elites at universities, are completely out of touch, have no idea what we're really complaining about." And for me . . . This was by way of a lead-up to a question for Julian, because you were saying, Julian, that you really were unsurprised by what happened on January 6. Because I will say that I was suckered into believing, as I was watching, that, "Okay, good. Now it ends." Because for Nancy Pelosi[35] it was Epiphany. So we would just follow the Christian holiday of Epiphany. Okay. Now these Republicans who have been cropping up, they're

34 Cosplay is a portmanteau of "costume" and "play," meaning the practice of dressing up as a character from a film/anime, TV show, comic book / graphic novel / manga, or video game, most popularly, from the science fiction genre.
35 Nancy Pelosi (D-Calif.) was Speaker of the House between 2007 and 2011 and again between 2019 and 2023.

going to have to say, "Okay. We should never have said the election was stolen. That was a mistake. Turns out we really value Republican voters. This has gone too far."

MCCURRY: We got five minutes of that.

LEPORE: I genuinely thought that afternoon . . . I was like, "As bad as this is, I hope people don't die. But I hope this, at least, means that the veil is lifted and people can see this is why Trump is dangerous. This is why he needed to be impeached." And I thought that this would be clear. I thought he'd be impeached the next day. I thought—I thought that there's no way they could stitch that back together.

VARIOUS: And it's like it never happened.

ZELIZER: I was only surprised that there was a few minutes where some Republicans said—

MCCURRY: Really?

ZELIZER: Yeah . . . separated themselves from him. And it's a pretty consistent pattern, at least in four years. He did something outrageous. He did something dangerous. He did something that was not supposed to be done. And you always heard crickets and silence, other than Mitt Romney.[36] And I don't know. My instinct was different on that. I think I heard Kevin McCarthy[37] on some radio show on my phone in that cab ride [Uber ride on the sixth, when Zelizer heard about the events at the Capitol]. And even him, at that moment, they were like,

---

36 Mitt Romney served as the Republican governor of Massachusetts from 2003 to 2007 and was the Republican nominee for president in 2012. He was sworn in as a senator from Utah in 2019.

37 Kevin McCarthy (R-Calif.) was elected to Congress in 2006 and in 2018 was elected the House Republican leader. He was elected majority leader of the House of Representatives in January 2023, following a protracted series of ballots.

"Okay, Congressman McCarthy wants to make a statement about how bad all this is." But in that statement he instantly said, "We need to get rid of extremism on both sides: the left and the right." He went right to that standard rhetoric, which is halfway to "Nothing too bad happened here." We all have our extremists. And so . . . I don't know. That's the pattern. And this was all forecast. The only thing that surprised me is no one was ready to stop him. I say that as someone who believed this was moving in a very bad direction. Yet it still, at some level, surprises and shocks. And we still don't have a full account of that. The trouble was brewing. We knew trouble was growing. Even these protests—

MCCURRY: Well, they were ready for some things. They were ready for electoral fraud. It was impressive in the last election: watching the immediate mobilization of Democratic lawyers . . . Because that's messing with the works. They were ready for that. But I think they weren't ready . . . Nobody was ready for this assault on the Capitol. And I have the same reaction as you. And I literally think it's dragging on me. It's like a weight. It feels like it isn't over. There's no illusion that it's over. And what we're learning in the aftermath makes it even more disturbing. So the level of preparation, the level of planning—we don't know half of what we should know. And we might never find out. Because part of the reaction is—it's immediate. It's like the Klan hearings.[38] Democrats need half the members and they're going to

---

38 Congressional hearings were held to investigate the Ku Klux Klan in 1871. See Tiffany R. Wright, Ciarra N. Carr, and Jade W. Gasek, "Truth and Reconciliation: The Ku Klux Klan Hearings of 1871 and the Genesis of Section 1983," Dickinson Law Review 126, no. 3 (2022), https://ideas.dickinsonlaw.psu.edu/dlr/vol126/iss3/2.

call their witnesses. But they didn't even do that. I don't know where they got the balls to do that, to vote that down. It's because their own electorate won't punish them.

LEPORE: Eyewitnesses. They don't even need witnesses. They were there. I don't understand!

FREEMAN: I think, in that sense . . .

MCCURRY: Just write it down.

FREEMAN: I think in that sense, this moment, although it felt really different from everything else that came before, in one sense, there's a really strong thread of continuity. I'm like you, Julian, it did not surprise me at all that nobody stepped forward. Because there had been this spinelessness all along the way. So I had vain hope maybe a couple of people would step forward. I didn't expect it. But the reason why—and it's related to what you were both [Zelizer and McCurry] saying, which is there has been no accountability for anything that happened during the entire Trump administration. And accountability is democracy. If you're not holding people accountable, you're not going to have a functional democracy. You're just going to be inviting more of the same. So I totally agree with you, Stephanie. Of course it's not over. There's been no bounty. There's been no prize. There hasn't even been a real investigation yet. There's been not even a strong statement by a collection of members of Congress stepping forward and saying, "A line has been crossed, and we are using the bully pulpit of Congress to say, this can never happen again." Not Nancy Pelosi on her own, or some other member.

STURKEY: Yeah.

FREEMAN: There has been no line in the sand. And even a committee or an investigation that reveals all the details, all the things we don't know—even if it does that and there's no concrete result, that, in and of itself, is a moment of accountability. It shows what people did and how they did it. And, I think, in a democratic form of government that matters enormously. And we don't have that. And without that, I think we remain under attack.

DOWNS: That reminds me of what you, Joanne, said. I don't know if it was your podcast *Now and Then* about the Nazi trial.[39] A guy who's 102 years old or something. He's a Nazi.

FREEMAN: Yeah.

DOWNS: And you make a similar argument.

FREEMAN: We did.

DOWNS: He still has to be tried . . .

FREEMAN: We did.

DOWNS: . . . for the process of accountability, even though he's 102. So, there is that analogy.

FREEMAN: Precisely. That accountability matters, even though all of these hearings and committees often don't result in concrete change. But the fact that they happen, I think, matters enormously to the public as to how they understand what's allowable and what isn't and what they are entitled to want and have as citizens of the United States.

ZELIZER: You expect a lack of accountability when the party being investigated controls the machinery of government. So it's not a total surprise. Even though control of Congress has flipped, there still won't be the kind of accountability we hoped for as a result of the power of the minority, which relies on the

39 Heather Cox Richardson and Joanne Freeman, "Treason(ish)," August 17, 2021 in *Now and Then*, produced by CAFÉ and the Vox Media Podcast Network, podcast, 52 mins., https://podcasts.apple.com/us/podcast/treason-ish /id1567665859?i=1000532243571.

filibuster and other procedural mechanisms. Moreover, even with Democrats controlling the machinery, there still hasn't been accountability. So it's a pretty big problem. I agree with Joanne on that. And that is a lesson that is not unique to January 6. And I think January 6 just showed how far you can go for the president to go out and say "I love you" to them as this is going on, which—that's mind-blowing.[40] And nothing happens.

DOWNS: I want to raise some more questions that bring us back to how January 6 connects to the practice of history—particularly to the notion of a "useable past"—and how the storming of the Capitol can matter in these debates. In this context, does history have any kind of utility? When we think about the question of history's utility in political debates or in our own efforts to construct a useable past, we ought to ask the question of who the audience is for these analyses. Because for certain minorities, there is a central need for a useable past—especially for LGBT communities or for Black people; the historians in those communities have really central roles in shaping a cultural identity and how they understand their roots. And it brings me, then, to the Confederate flag in the Capitol. Because I think there's something at work there, and I want to hear what—

ZELIZER: Could I jump in on that?

DOWNS: Yes.

ZELIZER: I kind of agree. I think: (a) the audience does matter. And I think there are certain audiences—like those holding a Confederate flag and talking about why the 1619 Project is the end of the world. History is not going to be . . . It's not like we're

---

40 For an example, see President Trump Video Statement on Capitol Protesters, C-Span, January 6, 2021, https://www.c-span.org/video/?507774-1/president -trump-video-statement-capitol-protesters.

going to go out and have a seminar and all of a sudden their views will change. They don't care about that history. And there's other publics like that. And so I'm not sure, realistically, there's much persuading to be done. And this is a broader political phenomena. There's not persuading to be done as much as there was in other years. There's less public dialogue. And that includes history. I think the media, actually—it's not just a vehicle to talk about history. It's a target of trying to inject historical discussion. I don't know if it is as unsuccessful as you're [McCurry] saying. Jill, you've had an immense influence. You are out there. I can't tell you how many reporters I've talked to who ask, "You know Jill Lepore? I love her book." And I think there are other examples of that, either through books, or through op-eds, or through TV—whatever your medium. Podcasts. There's a lot of good work out there that is getting out there. And I think the media is cognizant of scholarship. Some, like Jamelle [Bouie], will actually use it in pretty remarkable fashion. There's people, the *New Yorker*, who will reference work. For others who are not as interested, even if it's cursory, it's better they're hearing some of it. Even a comparison that's not that useful, but at least says, "Hey, we had George Wallace in 1968. We had a lot of support with pretty violent, over-the-top stuff." There's some value to that. Same with politicians. A lot don't want to listen. A lot couldn't care less about what a historian has to say. But it's still valuable that it's part of the conversation. And then the other publics are our students. A lot of students in this country, who are hearing what historians do in the classroom. They're hearing it and reading it through our books. And whatever the "general public" is that reads all this stuff, they're still there. It's not an insignificant public. They are sizable. And so I think there's a way to have an effect as a historian. But I think you can't approach it [like] you're going to change the world.

DOWNS: Right.

ZELIZER: There are some people I know who think they can do that. And I think that's frustrating. I think all you can do is take what you know, take the work that you've done or the work that you've read, and, in whatever platform, put it out there. And, I don't know, I think that's the limit of what we can do. But that's valuable. I think it's good to have it. But in the end, I also agree with you [McCurry] that there's going to be limits. Not just in the media. Politicians, they never want to hear, really, from historians, because we give long-winded answers to questions when they need a one-paragraph memo: "What do I do now?" So they don't want Julian Zelizer: "Oh, let me tell you about the history of taxation." They want an economist to say, "Do X or Y." They also live in a polarized world where it is hard to shift perspectives—even if you want to. And so I think we have to accept those limits. But I think there's good work. The work on race, for instance, is amazing work that's now come out on the history of institutional racism, on protest politics, including your work, Elizabeth. It has been so valuable to the discussions about criminal justice. Does it change the response in the end in terms of policy? Does it affect laws? I don't know. Probably not. And my work is the same. But it's out there. And I think that's what we do.

FREEMAN: I think it matters. I think it matters. And I totally agree with you [Zelizer]. We're not going to change the world. But I totally agree.

ZELIZER: And occasionally, like with 1619, someone finds it and puts it out there. Look, I'm in a department with two different people in the 1619 debate: Sean and Kevin.[41] But the debate itself was valuable. Look, if you're one of the protesters in the Capitol, it's not of value. But just to have a debate about slavery, and race, and the origins of this country . . . I thought that was really a healthy thing to see. So I guess I'm just speaking about different audiences and proponents.

STURKEY: Look, one of my problems is that [the media] seem to be asking us trivial bullshit. So you go on TV, you write an op-ed. It's a formula. "When did this happen before?" And you give them the dates, and the basics, and make the comparisons. Well, we need to go to another level, where people like Arthur Schlesinger Jr.[42] was in cabinet or advising presidents. It's like, okay, based on that, what do we do next? So I know where I could make the argument that January 6 reflected Wilmington 1898 in a certain number of ways. "Okay, that's interesting." But then that's when I get shut off. But what they should be asking is, "Okay, Professor Sturkey, then what do we do next based on that information?" Because we have counties, and government buildings, and things like that named for people who participated in this Wilmington insurrection. Big names for

---

41 Sean Wilentz and Kevin Kruse are professors of history at Princeton University. Kruse contributed an essay to the 1619 Project and Wilentz has been one of the project's most vocal critics. See Kevin Kruse, "How Segregation Caused Your Traffic Jam," New York Times, August 14, 2019, https://www.nytimes.com /interactive/2019/08/14/magazine/traffic-atlanta-segregation.html; Sean Wilentz, "A Matter of Facts," *The Atlantic*, January 22, 2020, https://www .theatlantic.com/ideas/archive/2020/01/1619-project-new-york-times-wilentz /605152/.

42 Arthur Schlesinger Jr. (1917–2007) was an influential Pulitzer Prize–winning American historian and Harvard professor. He was a member of President John F. Kennedy's cabinet, the special assistant to the president. He was awarded the National Humanities Medal in 1998.

Confederates—it's no surprise that the Confederate flag was in the Capitol. We fully embraced the Confederacy as a country, especially in the South. All is forgiven for many people. But because of that, we need to bury January 6. The left needs to absolutely bury it and run against it. Not just in the next election; not just in 2024, but ten, fifteen, twenty years down the road. To show those highlights. And not just hold people accountable through legislation, but culturally, with documentaries, with highlight reels of what that was. It needs to never go away. I think that it's one thing to say about the right, Trump: holding people accountable for it. But the left can also run against it constantly. And I think that Donald Trump in 2016 was, in many ways, still running against Bill Clinton in the nineties. And I think the left could very much do the same thing. You make your boogeyman. That's your boogeyman. And you run against that, basically, for the next twenty years.

HINTON: I want to respond to something that Julian said. Because it may be true that we will not change the world. But I think the best history is the history that seeks to change the world. I think, to Jill's point, part of the problem is that we're so insular. Many of us, not those of us in this room, but many of our colleagues, speak to rooms with only other experts. And the work that we must do more of moving forward, if we're going to get to the root of any of these problems is to reckon with our history . . . especially compared to other nations. We have not reckoned with our history at all. And so that's why you need historians to really step up and help us reckon with that history. So whether its aim is to change the world or reach a wide audience. Because I think that's the other thing that's so clear—and so clear from that electoral map on November 8—is that we must change our educational system, the information that people are getting. That comic book version of the Revolution that they're getting. And that's up to us. And so, this is important to me, that more of us seek these larger goals, even if we won't get there or write in these traditions.

MCCURRY: The connection between the fights over the history and then education policy itself, or the law, the outlawing of certain kinds of discussions: historians have been on the line about these things before. Sheldon Hackney and people like that around the NEH . . .[43] And so it seems to me we're in one of those moments. And historians are called to testify in congressional panels and so forth. [Kathleen] Belew was there on one of the panels recently. So there are ways. I'm not trying to say that . . . I was actually just responding more to the question that it's really all about the media. Because I think, for example, politicians, you don't reach.

LEPORE: Will just made an incredibly powerful political consultancy argument. You don't think that—

MCCURRY: No, I'm about to say, I actually think that there's been an enormous impact on policy, of stuff on race and health, for example. It took about two days, when the pandemic started, for the recognition to be made that this is disproportionately affecting low-income people, who are predominantly people of color. And where does that come out of? Dorothy Robert's work. And Alondra Nelson is one of Biden's policy people. I think there is a

43 Sheldon Hackney (1933–2013 was an award-winning historian of the American South who taught at Princeton before serving as president of both Tulane University and the University of Pennsylvania. He served as chair of the National Endowment of the Humanities from 1993 to 1997.

lot of policy input, actually.[44] And I think even the Reparations Bill is drawing on all kinds of information about historic structures of injustice. But we're in a tough moment in terms of history teaching. It's not like the humanities are growing. And also I'm sure Joanne lives in this world. The people that need a different version of history are reading the *Founding Brothers* forty times.[45] And even at Columbia, there's a lot of students who come to me with that kind of stuff. That's what they think history is. So I think our work is definitely cut out for us. And I'm certainly not saying that we shouldn't make our views known and engage in these arguments. I actually am a little bit worried about how the arguments among historians about 1619 and 1776 go, because it just feels like a food fight. And I—

DOWNS: What do you mean? Spell it out.

MCCURRY: No, I just think that it's ridiculous. It pits a small group of historians against another small group of historians.[46]

---

44 Alondra Nelson, *Body and Soul: The Black Panther Party and The Fight Against Medical Discrimination* (Minneapolis: University of Minnesota Press, 2013); Alondra Nelson, *The Social Life of DNA* (Boston: Beacon, 2016); Dorothy Roberts, *Fatal Invention: How Science, Politics, and Big Business Re-create Race in the Twenty-First Century* (New York: New Press, 2012).

45 McCurry is likely referring to Joseph Ellis, *Founding Brothers: The Revolutionary Generation* (New York: Vintage, 2002).

46 For examples of the debate over whether slavery caused the American Revolution, see Sean Wilentz, "A Matter of Facts," *The Atlantic*, January 22, 2020, https://www.theatlantic.com/ideas/archive/2020/01/1619-project-new -york-times-wilentz/605152/; "We Respond to the Historians Who Critiqued the 1619 Project," New York Times, December 20, 2019, https://www.nytimes .com/2019/12/20/magazine/we-respond-to-the-historians-who-critiqued-the -1619-project.html; Leslie Harris, "I Helped Fact-Check the 1619 Project. The Times Ignored Me," Politico, March 6, 2020, https://www.politico.com/news /magazine/2020/03/06/1619-project-new-york-times-mistake-122248. See also Janine Giordano Drake and Robert Cohen, "Debating the 1619 Project,"

STURKEY: Over two sentences in the project, largely.

MCCURRY: And they're there fighting it out. And to everybody's point today, if there was really a genuine discussion about that, it would be about the relationship between documents, and evidence, and argument—interpretation and argument. There's an act of choosing the evidence and an act of interpretation involved. And so what are we going to say about 1619? It's silly. It's like a thumbs-up, thumbs-down mode of engagement, which I really don't enjoy. And I feel like people are getting dragged into this and they should not be.

LEPORE: Yeah, I would just say, with all respect, I really disagree. I don't think it's a productive conversation at all. I think, actually, it's something that never gets mentioned in it because, of course, that project relies on the incredible revolution in academic historical research from the transformation of the academy during the 1960s that the *New York Times* did not review. The *New York Times* wins all these Pulitzers. Someone at the *New York Times* discovers American history involves racial strife and injustice. You're like, "Okay, well." When Sam Tanenhaus was running the *New York Times* Book Review, all they ever reviewed was David McCullough.[47] So it makes me furious that . . . The people whose work lies behind that project are to be celebrated and have been ignored. And their careers have been derailed by the lack of attention that the publishing industry, and the book

---

Social Education 86 (February 1, 2022), https://www.socialstudies.org/system /files/2022-02/se-8601009.pdf.

47 Sam Tanenhaus was book review editor of the *New York Times* from 2004 to 2013. American author and historian David McCullough (1933–2022) was awarded two Pulitzer Prizes (1993, 2002) as well as the National Book Award (1978), and indeed, his publications were always reviewed and nearly always well received in the Times.

review industry, and the prize-granting industry failed to give to them. And it's mostly scholars of color, who did really important archival work and wrote incredibly important books. And now the *New York Times* walks away with all the prizes that they should have won. It makes me crazy. And so for historians to have a little pissing match is incredibly discouraging about the nature of intellectual life in the country as a whole. It's not, to me, a celebration of how we can have great disagreements. It's just about the impoverishment of public discourse.

MCCURRY: It's also about striving for public attention and media space. That, I don't like. That's the thing I don't like most. So you give up this much and then . . . It's like a gladiator match. Throw twelve people into the ring, or four on each side. I think it's very unbecoming, actually, in the nineteenth-century sense of the word.

FREEMAN: I think it also gets back to framing. I agree with you, Julian. I think it's amazing that some of this debate is happening some of the time in some of the ways it's happening. But I think reducing this to 1619 or 1776 does an enormous disservice. . . . And that's often what it boils down to, these two dates, for some people.

LEPORE: There really isn't a world of scholarship that takes one side—

FREEMAN: No, no! That's what I mean. It's that that framing does a disservice to the conversation we ought to be having. And does precisely what you [Lepore] just said, which is all of these people who've done all of this scholarship that makes such a complex conversation, has so much to say, that's swept away by, well, "Is this one thing true or not? And what does that say about 1619?"

LEPORE: But the thing that, really, in terms of the changing the world piece . . . So I wrote my history of the United States, knowing I was going to be slaughtered by historians for doing it. Because Newt Gingrich's *[To] Renew America* was animated by his history book, which went out on satellite television.[48] You've got this renewing American civilization. It was a course online. You could watch it on TV. You could get the audio cassettes. You could get it with the GOPAC tapes.[49] He created a whole political movement around the reinterpretation of American history that no one was able to counter in public sphere.[50] And before I did it. And then the sixth happened, and I'm like, "I'm going to have to write a new chapter." So I've been struggling since the sixth to add this chapter. It's very hard to write a chapter that goes from Trump's election, which is where the book previously ended, to January 6. And part of me just keeps wishing that what, say, the OAH [Organization of American Historians] had been doing since January 6 was compiling an archive and putting together a commission of historians to write the history of that day. Okay, yes, it would be great if they . . . They should have their own commission, as Congress. But I think the moment it became clear when Rep. Kevin McCarthy started wobbling that that wasn't going to be happening.

MCCURRY: And they're going to cover this up.

LEPORE: We're the ones who were sitting holding these endowed professorships of American history while the country is literally

---

48 Newt Gingrich, *To Renew America* (New York: Harper Collins, 1995).

49 GOPAC is a Republican state and local political training organization.

50 Newt Gingrich, *To Renew America*; Jill Lepore, *These Truths: A History of the United States* (New York: Norton, 2018).

burning. And democracy is dying. Why are we not as a guild saying, "Let's build an archive?" Get some money. We could get a lot of jobs for a bunch of people to wade through the evidence, and we could write the 1/6 report.

HINTON: A bunch of graduate students who can't get jobs.

LEPORE: But seriously, what's more urgent . . . To your [Freeman] point of it has to be documented . . . There's accountability. There's also the political necessity. It is an active scholarly inquiry: figure out what the hell happened on that day. Why is that outside the bounds of—

MCCURRY: Who would convene it in your mind, Jill?

ZELIZER: Well, I think, if I could just jump in first on this. The OAH, the AHA [American Historical Association]—we have two major organizations, regional organizations. Certainly, we don't have to depend on being called in by politicians or the media to put out documentation, studies, or information about these kinds of events. This itself is an effort. But you could have organizational projects, initiatives to do this kind of stuff. Doesn't have to be connected to the left. There's different ways to think about it. There's been efforts to do it. I think the AHA has done some of this. But on something like January 6, I think you could easily put together historians to do some interesting project in real time. I'm just going to push back: I don't disagree on how the fight has been conducted. I also realize there were important and significant mistakes in parts of the [1619] text. I don't disagree on how the project takes the credit for lots of historians who have done this. But, at least in my experience, and it's just my experience, a debate like the one we have had on 1619 opens the door to a discussion of an issue—no one had ever asked me about it. When you do a group discussion, or you speak in front of or talk informally to educated people about where slavery fit in the evolution of the country—that, if framed well and handled well, there is a value. That doesn't mean go on Twitter and follow that stuff. But it creates a space by putting that out there that I think still . . .

DOWNS: Right.

ZELIZER: It might be misused, but we benefit from the discussion. And it's—

MCCURRY: I 110 percent agree with that, but I don't think that that's what's going on. I think that . . .

ZELIZER: Well, I give these talks, mostly on Zoom these days, and people were often asking genuinely about this. Some had a predisposition of where they stood. But they were at least asking. And they were like, "What's an example of the long-term impact of slavery?" And I could talk about Robin Einhorn's work in a group that would never give me the [opportunity] to talk about something like this.[51] So that's all I meant by that. And I still think that's part of the contribution—which is what I originally meant—of what historians can do if they're good at it. Sometimes it depends on other people picking it up. Sometimes it depends on being done in a crass fashion. But then historians step up in whatever outlets they have, and groups they have, and do it well. This is what I've tried to do. I work in a policy school too, where I'm literally teaching people who have been in the White House and Congress. So I believe in this. I just think you can't go into it with the expectation you will change the world. You could have the hope. But that can't be the only reason you

51 Robin Einhorn writes on the history of American taxation and the effect slavery has on contemporary attitudes toward taxation. See *American Taxation, American Slavery* (Chicago: University of Chicago Press, 2006).

do it. Because I think, often, historians will be frustrated then. And I worry if that is the expectation—(a) they'll quit quickly doing this, as opposed to seeing where the interventions lead; and (b) you can easily be seduced by bad incentives if you want to change the world. And I could tell you a million tricks to get on television as many times as you want. You just have to say the right thing in some ways. Or to get to testify. Some very good people testify . . . Often politicians are calling in people who will give them certain kinds of information. And that's a bad seduction, because then you're not making an intervention. You're giving talking points. And so you have to be willing to make certain argument and commit to doing it. But you might never see the effects. You might say things that are going to get you out of the political and public sphere. But if you do it with that mentality, I think that is changing the world. And that's the best way to make a contribution. That's all I think, if that makes sense.

FREEMAN: I'll be bluntly honest. I think, as a historian, I do op-eds, and webcasts, and podcasts, everything else because I don't know what I would do with myself if I didn't feel like I was doing something to help. Honestly, it kind of destroys me that I can't do more. So do I want people to hear what I'm saying? Do I want it to change some minds? Yes. Do I want to get the information out there? Yes. Do I hope that enough people will hear that, that it might make some difference? Yes, I do. But I honestly feel that I couldn't not do what I'm doing. Because I honestly feel that, as a historian who addresses the public constantly, without January 6, it would be a failure on my part to not step forward and do something. In a sense, for me, it's as emotional as my watching January 6, is the fact that I feel that—at this point in our country's history, where we are, and where that comes from, and where we might be going—how can we not step forward and say something? So, to me, that ends up being my biggest goading to do this. That's it.

DOWNS: We should be ending soon, but I did have a follow-up question for you, Joanne: A lot of historians engage the public for different reasons. Some use history to inform policy, some offer historical analysis in court cases. Some just love to teach the public. Why people want to engage the public often influences how they engage the public as intellectuals—some are didactic but sassy, others are snarky but informative. Some are just downright cantankerous. But in terms of your orientation, do you feel that your job is to explain things, like checks and balances, or to give context? Where are you . . . Because I follow you on Twitter and I've listened to, obviously, everything you say. You're not cantankerous.

FREEMAN: No. I'm deliberately not.

DOWNS: That's what I wanted to ask. That's what I'm trying to get at. Your point is to just—

FREEMAN: Inform. But I'm really deliberately not confrontational and cantankerous, because a lot of people follow me on Twitter and are listening to me—webcasts and podcasts—who are very right wing in their politics, and who I really don't agree with and they really don't agree with me. And if I beamed into public space with what I think, they will never hear me. But if I beam in and say, "Here's a way of looking at this, and here's how historically this way makes sense. And if you think about it this way, you might think differently." I've seen people who really don't agree with me, politically, change their mind.

DOWNS: Right.

FREEMAN: So I'm very deliberately diplomatic because I think I will reach people who don't agree with me that way.

DOWNS: That's fascinating. So I think we're really at time. This conversation is going to lead to a book that was initially titled "Insurrections." After I read Jill's article, "What Should We Call January 6?" in the *New Yorker*, I thought we shouldn't call it that because it assigns a particular way of interpreting January 6 and potentially depletes other interpretative possibilities. So I'm pushing away from that. Based on our lively, generative discussion on the place of historical analysis in larger debates, I've realized the book might be called "January 6 and the Politics of History." I feel the discussion just took a completely different turn . . . We can play with the title, by the way.

VARIOUS: Agreed.

DOWNS: So on that note, thank you so much. I am going to turn over to Catherine Clinton, co–series editor of History in the Headlines, who has silently observed this marvelous conversation, for the final word.

CATHERINE CLINTON: The book is called "a conversation." And that's important, that we thank you for your conversation. And I would like to say, I helped start this series because I love listening to these conversations. They stimulate a dozen more books. But I do want to end by saying, where I am now, I think globally and locally . . . So globally. I'm thinking about the fact that I got called by a BBC producer to talk about the 1619 moment. And that made me think about how all the wonderful work being done in this country to change ways of thinking about elections, takeovers—whether it's an insurrection, an uprising, a riot—reversing. . . . The way Elizabeth is saying, "Let's look at this event." And Jill quoted it, "This isn't a race riot. It's a white supremacy riot." Thinking carefully about the words we choose to describe January 6 will shape how the rest of the world understands it. So locally, I am thinking about teaching U.S. history in Texas. I teach in San Antonio, Texas, which serves many first-gen students and students of color. The state of Texas is a place where one in eleven schoolchildren will be getting their education in the United States. And I'm just wondering if any of you can give us a final comment on how we get this information into textbooks, and how we will make it a part of our everyday history when there are so many proposed laws restricting content.[52]

STURKEY: I don't have an answer. But this new Texas law, it seems they're this close [holds up thumb and pointer finger to indicate an inch] to banning primary sources. Because if you read the Ordinance of Secession in Texas, they don't mention state's rights—go figure—and slavery is everywhere. It's very obvious. They say such vile things all over Texas primary sources. And that discussion has been outlawed, basically, in so many public schools. It really seems to me that's the next logical step if they want to really get rid of those conversations. Just an observation.

FREEMAN: But wouldn't the documents actually help with those conversations? Because then it's not you introducing it.

ZELIZER: Yeah, but they counter the right.

MCCURRY: They violate the rule that they've set down. That's the issue. Could that be a legal challenge to it? I don't know. This is very untested. And when I was thinking about our meeting

---

52 See, for example, Brian Lopez, "Republican Bill That Limits How Race, Slavery and History Are Taught in Texas Schools Becomes Law," *Texas Tribune*, December 2, 2021, https://www.texastribune.org/2021/12/02/texas-critical-race-theory-law/#:~:text=Republican%20bill%20that%20limits%20how ,public%20policy%20or%20social%20affairs.%E2%80%9D.

today, and our conversation, and this long history, I just kept thinking about that abortion law. That bizarre abortion law.[53]

FREEMAN: Vigilante.

MCCURRY: Some lawyer was talking about municipal. It started as part of the municipal code. And then he scaled it up [to state law] when he was invited to. So these things are so linked in this moment. And the crackdown on progressive views of the past—any serious reference to slavery or racial exploitation—gone. And the position of women. That is basically what's being put out there, is, "Who cares what you think or need?" Literally, who speaks for who here? So I think those are very connected things. The history serves their view of the politics of the moment. And it's pretty awful from lots of positions, including race and gender.

ZELIZER: It's very dire. That's an area where, again, we started with January 6, but we should be cognizant of how far this could go. I think that, not just Texas, some of these other state efforts and laws are consequential. And the most basic level of history education starts in primary and secondary education. And I think historians, as an organization, certainly must be very vocal about this, whether it's through [teaching] or through other public efforts. I think that is an area where historians of all words and different kinds of history have to be very vocal about why this is

53 Texas statue S.B. 8—called the "Heartbeat Act"—incentivizes individuals to bring lawsuits against anyone who provides abortion care or assists someone in obtaining an abortion in violation of the ban on termination of a pregnancy after six weeks. The law took effect September 1, 2021. The U.S. Supreme Court declined to block this law—and a ruling handed down by the Texas Supreme Court in February 2022 determined that it would stand. See Rhae Lynn Barnes and Catherine Clinton, eds., *Roe v. Wade: Fifty Years Later* (Athens: University of Georgia, forthcoming), another History in the Headlines series volume.

so dangerous. I don't know if it will make a difference. And so that's back to the persuadable problem. I think they don't really care. But Texas is not all one [type]. And there's a lot of different pockets of Texas that won't be on board with this. And that's what you're trying to nurture. Again, it doesn't have to be a left-right. It must be almost an anticensorship, about a full education posture. That I think is really vital.

ZELIZER: This is another, different kind of crossroads: that we can't let the classroom be impoverished this way. Because then all the other things we've talked about today are really irrelevant. Because if you have students just learning skewed, fake history—cooked—[then] by the time they get to college, we have a big problem on our hands.

LEPORE: I think there are a lot of ways to try to respond. I'm not that optimistic about whether they'll succeed. I've written something about the Florida law. But I've also been revising my *These Truths* book for a collegiate edition.

MCCURRY: Good for you.

LEPORE: Which is just to be something that's available that's very cheap. Even the trade book is twenty bucks. Ten bucks used. So I don't know. I don't want say it's not the most fun I've had writing that book, but I felt like—

MCCURRY: Turning it into a textbook.

LEPORE: Turning it into a textbook is not super fun.

MCCURRY: No, nobody likes that, but good for you. But when I taught in California ... Jill and I were actually colleagues briefly in UC, San Diego. But there was an ongoing program, which I think it was called the California History Project, and it was K–12. And university faculty who needed money taught it in the summer. And it got taken apart at a certain point. But it's a budget issue, it's a money issue. And we have so many unemployed people who want to work in our discipline. There used to be presidential commissions that historians were invited to be part of. Alice Kessler Harris and Linda Kerber and all these people were on the President's Commission on the Status of Women.[54] And there was a real connection there. Really generative for everybody. And they were pushing and fighting back against the anti-ERA thing . . . I think about that a lot. I don't know a lot about that period. I think, was it mid-seventies? But this is, I think, where we ought to be right now, with more direct ways to insist on an accounting of events and the collection of documents. I think that's just indispensable.

DOWNS: What a great note to end on! Thank you, everyone!

54 President John F. Kennedy established the President's Commission on the Status of Women in 1961. It was a twenty-two-month study designed to identify the barriers that prevented women from achieving basic rights. See "Commissions on the Status of Women Collection, 1967–1994," Schlesinger Library, Radcliffe Institute, https://id.lib.harvard.edu/ead/sch00350/. There was also an initiative created by the American Historical Association (AHA) in 1970 that historians like Alice Kessler-Harris and Linda Kerber participated in. On the aha, see Noralee Frankel, "Remembering the Rose Report," *Perspectives on History*, November 1, 2010, https://www.historians.org/research-and-publications/perspectives-on-history/november-2010/remembering-the-rose-report. Also, email from Alice Kessler-Harris to Jim Downs, January 3, 2019.

Top Ten Articles

Many of the topics covered in the roundtable are highlighted in the opinion pieces that follow. The "top ten" selection herein is by no means exhaustive nor definitive. The bibliography includes further resources regarding this topic, as does the series website for History in the Headlines (www.ugapress.org/index.php/series/HIH/).

What Should We Call the Sixth of January?

JILL LEPORE

New Yorker, January 8, 2021

"Big protest in D.C. on January 6th," Donald Trump tweeted before Christmas. "Be there, will be wild!" On New Year's Day, he tweeted again: "The BIG Protest Rally in Washington, D.C. will take place at 11:00 A.M. on January 6th." On January 5: "I will be speaking at the SAVE AMERICA RALLY tomorrow on the Ellipse at 11AM Eastern. Arrive early—doors open at 7AM Eastern. BIG CROWDS!" The posters called it the "Save America March." What happened that day was big, and it was wild. If it began as a protest and a rally and a march, it ended as something altogether different. But what? Sedition, treason, a failed revolution, an attempted coup? And what will it be called, looking back? A day of anarchy? The end of America?

Trump called the people who violently attacked and briefly seized the U.S. Capitol building in order to overturn a Presidential election "patriots"; President-elect Joe Biden called them "terrorists." In a section of *Leviathan* called "Inconstant Names," Thomas Hobbes, in 1651, remarked that the names of things are variable, "For one man calleth Wisdome, what another calleth Feare; and one Cruelty, what another Justice." On the other hand, sometimes one man is right (those people *were* terrorists). And, sometimes, what to call a thing seems plain. "This is what the President has caused today, this insurrection," Mitt Romney, fleeing the Senate chamber, told a *Times* reporter.

By any reasonable definition of the word (including the Oxford English Dictionary's: "The action of rising in arms or open resistance against established authority"), what happened on January 6 was an insurrection. An insurrection is, generally, damnable: calling a political action an insurrection is a way of denouncing what its participants mean to be a revolution. "There hath been in Rome strange insurrections," Shakespeare wrote, in *Coriolanus*. "The people against the senators, patricians, and nobles." Insurrection, in Shakespeare, is "foul," "base and bloody." In the United States, the language of insurrection has a vexed racial history. "Insurrection" was the term favored by slave owners for the political actions taken by people held in human bondage seeking their freedom. Thomas Jefferson, in the Declaration of Independence, charged the king with having "excited domestic insurrections amongst us." The English lexicographer Samuel Johnson, an opponent of slavery, once offered a toast "To the next insurrection of the negroes in the West Indies." And Benjamin Franklin, wryly objecting to southern politicians' conception of human beings as animals, offered this rule to tell the difference between them: "sheep will never make any insurrections."

The term's racial inflection lasted well beyond the end of slavery. In the nineteen-sixties, law-and-order Republicans used that language to demean civil rights protests, to describe a political movement as rampant criminality. "We have seen the gathering hate, we have heard the threats to burn and bomb and destroy," Richard Nixon said, in 1968. "In Watts and Harlem and Detroit and Newark, we have had a foretaste of what the organizations of insurrection are planning for the summer ahead." In that era, though, "riot" replaced "insurrection" as the go-to racial code word: "riots" were Black, "protests" were white, as Elizabeth Hinton argues in an essential, forthcoming book, *America on Fire: The Untold History of Police Violence and Black Rebellion Since the 1960s.* "Yet historically," Hinton observes, "most instances of mass criminality have been perpetrated by white vigilantes hostile to integration and who joined together into roving mobs that took 'justice' in their own hands." This remains an apt description of what happened on January 6.

One possibility, then, is to call the Sixth of January a "race riot." Its participants were overwhelmingly white; many were avowedly white supremacists. A lot of journalists described the attack on the legislature as a "storming" of the Capitol, language that white-supremacist groups must have found thrilling. Hitler's paramilitary called itself the *Sturmabteilung,* the Storm detachment; Nazis published a newspaper called *Der Stürmer,* the stormer. QAnon awaits a "Storm" in which the satanic cabal that controls the United States will be finally defeated. So one good idea would be never, ever to call the Sixth of January "the Storming of the Capitol."

What words will historians use in textbooks? Any formulation is a non-starter if it diminishes the culpability of people in positions of power who perpetrated the lie that the election was stolen. It's not a coup d'etat because it didn't succeed. It's not even a failed coup, because a coup involves the military. And, as Naunihal Singh, the author of *Seizing Power: The Strategic Logic of Military Coups* told *Foreign Policy,* the word "coup" lets too many people off the hook. "The people who you want to point fingers at are the president, the party leaders, and the street thugs," Singh said. "And we lose that if we start talking about a coup; it gives a pass to all of the Republican politicians who have been endorsing what Trump's saying."

In truth, the language of the coop seems more appropriate than the language of the coup. I mean chickens. "Coming home to roost" quite aptly describes the arrival of armed terrorists in the hall where, moments before, Senator Ted Cruz had summoned that very flock as he stood on the floor and urged the legislature to overturn the election. Derrick Evans, the West Virginia Republican lawmaker who joined the mob and, as he breached the doors of the Capitol, cried out, "We're in! We're in!" acted with more honesty and consistency than the 147 members of the House and Senate who, later that night, voted to overturn the results of the election after having hidden, for hours, from the very people they'd been inciting for months and even years.

"Sedition" is too weak. Noah Webster, in his *American Dictionary of the English Language*, from 1828, offered this handy way to distinguish "sedition" from "insurrection": "sedition expresses a less extensive rising of citizens." In any case, "sedition," in the sense of a political rebellion, is obsolete. "Treason," an attempt to overthrow the government, seems fair, though it almost risks elevating what looked to be a shambles: a shabby, clownish, idiotic, and aimless act of mass vandalism. If I were picking the words, I'd want to steer very clear of ennobling it, so I'd be inclined to call it something blandly descriptive, like "The Attack on the U.S. Capitol," or "The Sixth of January."

"Remember this day forever!" Trump tweeted at one minute past six on Wednesday night. There's no danger that anyone will forget it, by whatever name. The harder question is not what to call the events of that day, but what to make of the maddening four years and more that led up to it: the long, slow rot of the Republican

Party; the perfidy of Republicans in the House and Senate since January, 2017; the wantonness of a conservative media willing to incite violence; the fecklessness of Twitter and Facebook; and, not least, the venality, criminality, and derangement of the President. Whether that story belongs under a chapter titled "The Rise and Fall of Donald J. Trump" or "The End of America" awaits the outcome of events.

What Trump Shares with the "Lost Cause" of the Confederacy

KAREN L. COX

New York Times, January 8, 2021

Wednesday morning, President Trump urged a crowd of supporters who showed up in Washington, D.C., to "walk down to the Capitol" and protest the certification of the election taking place nearby on Pennsylvania Avenue. A few hours later, he stood in the White House Rose Garden to deliver a different message after members of this same group—who carried flags bearing his name—stormed the Capitol, brawled with Capitol Police, and breached both chambers of Congress. Mr. Trump repeated false claims about election fraud but told them: "You have to go home now. We have to have peace."

As the Trump presidency comes to a close after a sound defeat, and after four years of having led a movement that many agree has undermined our Constitution and the nation itself, it is difficult not to see the parallels between his lost cause and the failed cause of the Confederacy in 1865. As individuals carried the flag of the Confederacy, the flag of rebellion against the United States, into the Capitol, it was a moment not lost on historians—and a moment of dire concern for most Americans.

Mr. Trump's feeble message to his stalwarts about going home and keeping the peace was similar in tone to Gen. Robert E. Lee's admonitions in the aftermath of defeat. "I think it wiser," he wrote, "not to keep open the sores of war, but to follow the examples of those nations who endeavored to obliterate the marks of civil strife."

Lee was referring to the creation of monuments, but he was essentially telling those who admired him to "go home" and keep the peace. Yet by the time he made those comments in 1869, the myth of the Lost Cause and its justifications for Confederate defeat were in full flower. And it was Lee—not President Jefferson Davis, whom many white Southerners blamed for their loss—that helped to personify the narrative of a just cause. He was a leader who had not failed the white South; rather, he had been failed by others. He was also the man they believed best represented the values of their cause.

Mr. Trump's lost cause mirrors that of Lee's. His dedicated followers do not see him as having failed them, but as a man who was failed by others. Mr. Trump best represents their values—even those of white supremacy—and the cause he represents is their cause, too. Just as Lee helped lead and sustain the Confederacy over four years, Mr. Trump has also been a sort of general—in a campaign of disinformation.

And if there was ever a campaign of disinformation, the Lost Cause was it. The Confederacy, the lie went, failed only because of the North's superior numbers and resources. But it went further than that. As Edward Pollard, the Richmond editor who coined the term "Lost Cause," wrote in 1866, "The Confederates have gone out of this war with the proud, secret, *dangerous* consciousness that they are the BETTER MEN, and that there was nothing wanting but a change in a set of circumstances and a firmer resolve to make them victors."

This constitutes another parallel to the movement Mr. Trump has created. Under a change in circumstances—overturning the results of the election—the better man would have won. This is the "dangerous consciousness" of Trump's supporters. Like Lee's Lost Cause, it will not likely end. When Lee died just five years after the Civil War, the myths around Confederate defeat and efforts to memorialize it were growing exponentially throughout the South. The Lost Cause did not belong to Lee; Lee belonged to the Lost Cause—a cultural phenomenon whose momentum could not be stopped.

Even if Mr. Trump were to remove himself from public life in the coming years, his lost cause and the myths he's helped create about elections, voter fraud, and fake news will likely continue, a cultural and political phenomenon that shows no sign of ending.

Like the original Lost Cause, today's movement has been aided and abetted by the president's field generals—many of them Republican members of Congress. They espouse the same language, stoke the same flames and perpetuate the same myths—all to incite a base of voters to keep them in office. It also ensures that the "sores of war," received in battles to restore white supremacy in the face of an increasingly diverse polity, not only remain but become gaping wounds that fester with racism, sexism, homophobia, and nativism.

There is a saying that the South lost the war but won the peace—that military defeat did not stop the Confederate cause and that the Lost Cause was not entirely lost. It was won through the rewriting of history, electing officials who sought to reestablish political and social control over freedmen and women, through violence and draconian legislation, and by perpetuating the mythology that theirs was a sacred cause and that white Southerners were a patriotic people who had done nothing more than to try to preserve states' rights.

Mr. Trump's tweet to his followers echoed these same sentiments. He referred to his cause as "sacred" and to those who supported him as "great patriots" and admonished them to "Remember this day forever!" This is how the original Lost Cause emerged, and if history repeats itself in the decades ahead, Trump Republicans will continue to defend what he began, think of it as a patriotic duty, and not only will they "never forget," they will most likely perpetuate these sentiments onto future generations.

This is how the myth of Lost Cause played out in the states of the former Confederacy. It grew in strength, found support among white Northerners, and has lasted for generations such that even today, more than 150 years later, people defend its basic tenets.

Mr. Trump's lost cause, however, is far more dangerous because it affects more than a region; it is national in scope. It has ensnared everyone from Senators Josh Hawley of Missouri and Ted Cruz of Texas, to over 130 Republican members of the House, to the Proud Boys and Women for Trump. Democrats may be able to win general elections, but Trumpism will live on in Republican-dominated legislatures whose members remain in power, in some cases at least, because of voting restrictions and district gerrymandering.

The constant refrain coming from Republican leaders is that the insurrection at the U.S. Capitol is "not who we are." And yet how else are we to explain what happened? If it is not who we are, then all members of both parties should reject this twenty-first century lost cause. But too many Republicans haven't—and unless they do, its impact could last for generations.

Dangers from the Enemy Within

ERIC FONER

The Nation, January 8, 2021

January 6, 2021, will long be remembered as the day two strands of the American experience, both deeply embedded in our national history, collided. One was reflected in the election of African American and Jewish senators from Georgia. This is a state that witnessed the 1915 lynching of the Jewish factory superintendent Leo Frank, the transformation of Tom Watson from a populist who sought to unite poor Black and white farmers into a vicious racist and anti-Semite, and the Atlanta Massacre of 1906, in which white mobs killed perhaps two dozen African Americans, not to mention the premiere in 1939 of the film *Gone With the Wind,* a paean to the Ku Klux Klan. The election results are the culmination of a mass, interracial movement to transform a state that long denied its Black population the right to vote into a genuine democracy. The campaign led by Stacey Abrams and others to register new voters is an inspiring example of the possibility of progressive change.

Yet the riot by supporters of President Trump, aimed at preventing the counting of electoral votes, reveals a darker side of the history of American democracy. One can begin with the fact that, more than two centuries since the adoption of the Constitution, we still select the president through the Electoral College, an archaic system that reflects the founders' conviction that ordinary people are not to be trusted with voting directly for president, and their desire to bolster the slaveholding South, whose political power was augmented by the three-fifths clause that gave slave states extra electoral votes based on their disenfranchised Black population. Indeed, Trump occupies the White House only because an undemocratic electoral system makes it possible to lose the popular vote and still become president. Moreover, efforts to restrict the right to vote by race, gender, or some other criteria have a long history. The idea that the people should choose their rulers, the essence of democracy, has always coexisted with the conviction that too many people—of the wrong kind—are casting ballots. Georgia's requirement that office seekers receive over 50 percent of the vote or face a runoff election, enacted in 1963 at the height of the civil rights revolution, was intended to prevent the victory of a candidate preferred by Blacks if several aspirants split the white vote.

The events of January 6 are the logical culmination of the disrespect for the rule of law nurtured by the Trump presidency, evidenced in the glorification of armed neo-fascist groups, most notoriously until now at Charlottesville; the whipping up of antimask and antilockdown riots in Michigan and other states; and the refusal to accept the clear results of the presidential election. But those familiar with American history know that the Capitol riot was hardly the first effort to overturn extralegally the results of a democratic election. The Reconstruction era and the years that followed witnessed many such events, some far more violent than the January 6 riot. Scores of members of a Black militia unit were murdered in 1873 in Colfax, Louisiana, by armed whites who seized control of the local government from elected Black officials.

An uprising the following year by the White League sought to overthrow the biracial Reconstruction government of Louisiana. (A monument to this effort to restore white supremacy stood for decades in New Orleans until removed in 2017 by Mayor Mitch Landrieu.) In 1898, a coup by armed whites in Wilmington, North Carolina, ousted the elected biracial local government. By the early twentieth century, Black voting and office holding had essentially ended throughout the South. This is not just ancient history. As recently as 2013, the Supreme Court eviscerated key provisions of the Voting Rights Act, opening the door to widespread efforts in Republican-controlled states to suppress the ability to vote. Let's not assume that until the Capitol riot the United States was a well-functioning democracy.

Alexander H. Stephens, the Georgia political leader who served as vice president of the Confederacy, famously described the effort to create a slaveholders' republic as an embodiment of the "great truth that the Negro is not equal to the white man, that slavery . . . is his natural and normal condition." January 6 may be the first time the Confederate flag was openly displayed in the Capitol building—a shocking sight that, I hope, will never be repeated. But in his opposition to the removal of monuments to Confederate leaders and to renaming military bases on the grounds that they erase "our" history, Trump has consciously identified his presidency with the Confederacy and the white nationalism at its core.

Today, the United States spends far more on its military than any other nation. Yet the mob that stormed the Capitol consisted not of Chinese, Iranians, Russians, or other purported enemies of American democracy but of our fellow citizens. Nearly two centuries ago, in his famous Lyceum speech, Abraham Lincoln condemned growing disrespect for the rule of law as the greatest danger to American democracy. "If destruction be our lot," he declared, "we must ourselves be its author and finisher." The results in Georgia and Trump's imminent departure from the presidency offer hope for a revitalization of a democratic political culture. But now, as in Lincoln's time, the danger to American democracy ultimately lies within.

How Trumpism May Endure

DAVID BLIGHT

New York Times, January 9, 2021

One hundred and fifty years after the emergence of the Confederate Lost Cause ideology, a new Lost Cause invaded the U.S. Capitol with the incitement of the president of the United States. Waving American, Confederate, Gadsden, and, especially, Trump flags, Donald Trump's loyalists desecrated the greatest symbolic edifice of America.

Trumpism has already become a lethal Lost Cause. It does not quite have martyrs and a cult of the fallen in which to root its hopes and dreams. But it does have a self-destructive cult leader about to leave power in a defeat that has been transformed into a narrative of betrayal, resistance, and a promise of political revitalization.

The important Lost Causes in history have all been at heart compelling stories about noble defeats that were, with time, forged into political movements of renewal: the French after the Franco-Prussian War of 1870–71 and the profound need for national *revanche;* Germany after the Great War and its "stab in the back" theory that led over the 1920s to the rise of the nationalism and racism of the Nazis; and the white South after our Civil War. All Lost Causes find their lifeblood in lies, big and small, lies born of beliefs in search of a history that can be forged into a story and mobilize masses of people to act politically, violently, and in the name of ideology.

The *story* demands a religious loyalty. It must be protected, reinforced, practiced in ritual, and infused with symbols. What is the Trumpian claim of a stolen election but an elaborate fiction that fights to make the reality and truth of the unbelievers irrelevant. Some myths are benign as cultural markers; but others are rooted in big lies so strong as engines of resentment that they can fill parade grounds and endless political rallies, or motivate the storming of the U.S. Capitol in a quixotic attempt to overthrow an election.

Mr. Trump's Lost Cause takes its fuel from conspiratorial myths of all kinds, rehearsed for years on Trump media and social media platforms. Its guiding theories include: Christianity under duress and attack; large corrupt cities full of Black and brown people manipulated by liberal elites; Barack Obama as alien; a socialist movement determined to tax you into subservience to "big government"; liberal media out to crush family and conservative values; universities and schools teaching the young a history that hates America; resentment of nonwhite immigrants who threaten a particular national vision; and whatever hideous new version of a civil religion QAnon represents.

An effective, enduring Lost Cause story needs to know clearly what it hates, has to attain widespread control of its own communication, and needs institutional rooting, and it must explain almost everything. It converts loss and longstanding grievance into community and promises of victory on altars of strife.

The Confederate Lost Cause is one of the most deeply ingrained mythologies in American history. It emerged first as a mood of traumatized defeat in the 1860s, but grew into an array of arguments, organizations, and rituals in search of a story that could win hearts and minds and regain power in the southern states. It was initially a psychological response to the trauma of collective loss among former Confederates. It gained traction in violent groups such as the Ku Klux Klan and in the re-emergence of the Democratic Party's resistance to Reconstruction.

It assumed the character of a religious movement in endless sermons about the noble fallen soldiers who defended home, hearth, their women, and their God. It maintained that the best cause in a war can lose nobly if overwhelmed by industrial might and other evil forces of modernity. A lasting civil religion requires a saint, and the South quickly created one out of the life of Robert E. Lee, the Confederacy's leading general who fought to the bitter end, but died in 1870, before he could discourage the ubiquitous mythmaking and monument building in his honor.

Crucially, the Lost Cause argued that the Confederacy never fought to preserve slavery, and that it was never truly defeated on battlefields. Lost Cause spokesmen saw the Confederacy as the true heir of the American Revolution, and maintained that loss by the underdog could transform into a success story even for Yankees in need of security and patriotic sentiment in an age of anxiety over rapid urbanization, immigration, and strife between labor and capital. Above all, the Lost Cause seductively reminded white Americans that the Confederacy had stood for a civilization in which both races thrived in their natural capacities, a regime of proper racial and gender order. The slaughter of the Civil War had destroyed that order, but it could be remade and the whole nation, defined as white Anglo-Saxon, could yet be revived.

By the 1890s, the Lost Cause was no longer a story of loss, but one of victory: the defeat of Reconstruction. Southerners—whether run-of-the-mill local politicians, famous former generals, or women who forged the culture of monument building—portrayed white supremacy and home rule for the South as the nation's victory over radicalism and Negro rule. Reconstruction in the 1860s, forged in the three great constitutional amendments (Thirteenth, Fourteenth, and Fifteenth), had been overthrown to the glory of America.

The Trumpian Lost Cause has quite different origins, of course. It does not derive from sacrifice of blood and treasure in war. On its face it is not a response to the military conquest of a society. But it does seem to be tonic for those who fear long-term social change; it is a story in search of revival and order. Trumpism knows what it hates: liberalism; taxation; what it perceives as big government; nonwhite immigrants who drain the homeland's resources; government regulation imposed on individuals and businesses; foreign entanglements and wars that require America to be too generous to strange peoples in faraway places; any hint of gun control; feminism in high places; the nation's inevitable ethnic and racial pluralism; and the infinite array of practices or ideas it calls "political correctness." Potent ideas all in search of a history.

Trumpists want something permanent and stable: border walls; ever-growing stock portfolios; access to the environment and hunting land without limits; coal they can burn at will; the "liberty" to reject masks; history that tastes of the sweetness of progress and not the bitterness of national sins. In his book *The End of the Myth: From the Frontier to the Border Wall in the Mind of America*, the historian Greg Grandin describes how a growing sense of alienation, grievance, and inequality led millions of largely white Americans to embrace the simple but clear story Mr. Trump told them. From more than a decade of angry right-wing attacks on all things Obama, Democratic Party, and liberal, they were primed for "a conspiratorial nihilism, rejecting reason and dreading change" as they tuned in to Rush Limbaugh, watched Fox News, and strolled down the internet rabbit hole to Q.

If, as many Civil War scholars have suggested, the Confederate Lost Cause was born in the imagery of Lee's manly and noble surrender to Ulysses Grant at Appomattox in April 1865, perhaps the Trump Lost Cause has been born in the indelible imagery of the rioters scaling and assaulting the U.S. Capitol in January 2021. Their story, however fraught with lies and misguided beliefs, has tremendous traction among a majority of sitting Republicans in Congress, in the constellation of right-wing media, and now in their thousands of veterans of the march on the Capitol. They may soon need a new high priest with much better political talent; there is no lack of candidates awaiting their chance.

Mr. Trump lost, but he and his minions may yet find ways, if they keep their deep foothold in the Republican Party, to manufacture a dreamlike story of future victory for their unstable coalition of an unhindered ruling class, Christian nationalism, and the aggrieved, white working class. Whether Trumpism can ever attain the staying power of the Confederate Lost Cause is unclear. It may flame out in a few years like the bad TV show it has always been. But the shock of Trumpists' inevitable attack on the American experiment on Wednesday, January 6, hit like a thunderbolt. They will be back. It will surely take great political skill and moral imagination across American culture, from the Biden administration to every teacher in the land, to fight this new Lost Cause ideology. The country needs healing and unity, but it needs justice and better storytelling of its history more.

The Supreme Court's *United States v. Stanley* decision in 1883 declared that the equal protection provision of the Fourteenth

Amendment could be enforced only by the states, effectively plac-
ing individual rights beyond federal protection. Frederick Douglass
reacted with outrage, saying the decision felt like a "moral cyclone."
He blamed it on a failure of historical memory in facing down the
power of the Lost Cause. Douglass spoke for Black Americans'
"bewildering surprise." "The surrender of the national capital to
Jefferson Davis in time of war," he asserted, "could hardly have
caused a greater shock." That Confederate flag parading inside the
Capitol on Wednesday caused similar national pain and shock.

A Line Was Crossed on January 6

We Need to Declare That Emphatically, Historian Writes, before It's Too Late

JOANNE B. FREEMAN

Washington Post, December 12, 2021

Nearly a year after the January 6 assault on the U.S. Capitol, with the duly elected president in place, it's tempting to conclude that the insurgency failed. It didn't. At least, not yet. Our government is still under attack. The offensive is quieter now but no less menacing, eroding the government from within. The fundamental right to vote is under siege. The regulation of elections is being corrupted. And faith in the electoral process is fading; the "big lie" about Donald Trump's supposed victory in 2020 has staying power for just that reason. Americans question the role and reliability of the Supreme Court and wonder whether they can trust health and safety institutions like the Centers for Disease Control and Prevention or the Food and Drug Administration—during a pandemic. For too many, the old idea that government is the enemy has a newly magnified appeal.

But the damage goes even deeper. Faith in democracy itself is slipping away. The stunningly muted response to the January 6 attack offers no comfort. More than seven hundred alleged rioters have been arrested, but their fates have varied; too many complicating factors prevent clear rulings of right and wrong, and sentences have been short and few.

It took a full six months for Congress to launch a formal investigation; five months later, the scope and purpose of the Select Committee to Investigate the January 6 Attack on the United States Capitol remain unclear. Its high-profile subpoenas have been mostly unanswered, resulting in one criminal indictment, that of former Trump strategist Stephen K. Bannon, and on Tuesday the committee announced that it would move to hold former Trump chief of staff Mark Meadows in contempt as well. The former Justice Department official Jeffrey Clark, who played a significant role in Trump's efforts to overturn the election, agreed to answer his subpoena on December 16, but he apparently plans to assert his Fifth Amendment rights so as not to incriminate himself.

Basic facts about the day's events and planning remain fuzzy. Journalists have offered a stream of revelations and allegations—the memo from lawyer John Eastman outlining a plan for overturning the presidential election; the report of a January 6 "war room" at the Willard Hotel; claims of dozens of planning sessions fostered by members of Congress—but each bombshell seems to vanish before it explodes.

Here's the problem, and it's foreboding: If a line is crossed, and the occasion passes unacknowledged, was there really a line? All these months after the attack, the seemingly bare-minimum response has not happened: There has been no full-throated group statement from the congressional bully pulpit declaring the attack out of bounds, no strong, clear line in the sand naming the events of January 6 an unforgivable assault on the democratic processes and principles of our government that must never happen again. This astounding omission could prove fatal.

Many Republicans have been doing the precise opposite of acknowledging a crossed line. They deny the attack's importance ("You would actually think it was a normal tourist visit," was how Representative Andrew S. Clyde characterized some of the footage), dismiss the need for an investigation ("Anything that gets us rehashing the 2020 elections," Senator John Thune said, is "a day lost") and stab at the probe's credibility ("This is a sham committee," House Minority Leader Kevin McCarthy, who may be the speaker by January 6, 2023, said of the bipartisan House panel). Even moderate Republicans have joined that chorus; on ABC's *The View* in October, former secretary of state Condoleezza Rice said she agreed with Senate Majority Leader Mitch McConnell that it was "time to move on."

New metal detectors in the Capitol—one of the few lasting additional protective measures—have met Republican resistance. Right wing pundits have claimed that the Capitol-Police officers who tearfully testified before the select committee this past July were "crisis actors" playing for effect. Some, including Trump himself, have transformed insurgent Ashli Babbitt, killed by law enforcement while trying to climb through a broken window inside the Capitol, into a martyred patriot. In the Senate, Republicans voted down the mere discussion of an investigation.

The message is clear: There's no reason to get upset. The day's events were unremarkable, perhaps even praiseworthy. Nothing more need be done.

This is dangerous. The nation suffered a deliberate attempt to violently overturn a free and fair election, with little pushback, an astonishing lapse that invites more of the same. Indeed, if there were Republican members of Congress involved—and despite a recent *Rolling Stone* report attributed to anonymous sources, there is no clear evidence that there were—they have retained their seats in violation of their oath of office, which requires them to "support and defend the Constitution of the United States against all enemies, foreign and domestic." The Constitution lays out the presidential electoral process; on January 6, 2021, domestic attackers tried to violate it. Full stop.

American history has ample examples of instances when a line was crossed and there was a firm, public repudiation of the offense. The health of our democracy has depended on it. Consider the caning of abolitionist senator Charles Sumner (R-Mass.). In May 1856, Sumner gave a two-day speech denouncing slavery generally and some of his pro-slavery antagonists in Congress specifically. Two days later, Representative Preston Brooks (D-S.C.), the kinsman of one of those enslavers, walked up to Sumner, who was seated at his Senate desk franking copies of his speech, and brutally caned him over the head, beating the bloody Sumner to the ground until the cane broke. At a time when sectional strife over slavery was peaking, the attack had a powerful national impact. Southerners sent Brooks fan mail and canes as tributes; Northerners voiced their outrage in mass "indignation meetings." North and South, Americans viewed the caning as the South beating the North into submission.

The official response was swift. The day after the caning, Congress formed an investigative committee. Although Democrats protested that it would further polarize the nation, the severity of the crime and its deliberate commission on the Senate floor carried the day. Those same factors led to a fiery House debate about the caning and its implications two months later—a debate so explosive that there were four near-duels in its aftermath.

In the end, the committee was divided over how to respond. Brooks resigned his seat in protest and was promptly reelected, only to die within months of a severe throat infection. After three years recovering from health problems caused by the caning, Sumner returned to the Senate and gave an even more savage anti-slavery speech. And the clash of North and South continued, help-ing pave the way to civil war.

But the post-Sumner proceedings did have an impact. They powerfully, publicly, and explicitly declared that a preplanned as-sault of a lawmaker on the floor of Congress was out-of-bounds. They taught southern congressmen that their northern colleagues would not back down in the face of such an attack. And equally if not more important, Congress had proved able and willing to defend itself and the democratic process. Lawmakers may not have agreed on a remedy, but they agreed on the severity of the offense.

The simple fact of a formal investigation has power, something Senator John Parker Hale (N.H.) appreciated as far back as 1850. On April 17 of that year, during debate on what would become the Compromise of 1850 over free and slave states, Senator Henry Foote (D-Miss.) grievously insulted Senator Thomas Hart Benton (D-Mo.), who was less bullish than Foote on the spread of slavery. When the outraged Benton lunged toward Foote, Foote grabbed a pistol from his pocket and pointed it at Benton. Mayhem en-sued. Some senators rushed for Foote's gun. Some tried to restrain Benton. Others jumped on desks and chairs to get a good look. Eventually, the chamber calmed and senators went back to work; this was hardly the first such congressional clash, or even the first threatened gunplay. But Hale wanted something more. A formal investigation was essential, he argued, not just for "vindicating the character of the Senate, but to set history right, and inform the public as to what *did* take place." The public needed to know what happened, and perhaps more important, they needed to see that Congress had taken the matter in hand. They needed to see the image—ideally, the reality—of Congress as a functioning institution. They needed to see the government holding itself accountable.

Accountability—the belief that political power holders are responsible for their actions and that blatant violations will be addressed—is the lifeblood of democracy. Without it there can be no trust in government, and without trust, democratic governments have little power.

The framers were well aware of this liability; it's why they were obsessed with the danger posed by demagogues, who seize power by pandering to the masses and winning their loyalty, toppling the old order in the process. Public accountability was one of many checks and balances the framers built into the Constitution to fend off that danger. It's one reason the Constitutional Convention rejected the idea of an executive council leading the nation, rather than a single president: In a council, a power-hungry wrongdoer could hide his crimes behind his colleagues. Better to have a single executive who would be restrained by the threat of public exposure and accountability. At least, such was their hope.

In the past, we've seen the impact of public exposure of a crossed line, even when it's slow to come. Senator Joseph McCarthy (R-Wis.) had been red-baiting the powerful and prominent for years before the televised 1954 hearings investigating alleged communism in the army. When McCarthy savagely lashed out at a young colleague of the army's chief counsel, Joseph Welch, Welch shot back: "Have you no sense of decency, sir?"—and moments later the spectators burst into applause. The line, at last, had been publicly acknowledged, eroding McCarthy's hold on power in the process. Later that year, he was censured for acts that "tended to bring the Senate into dishonor and disrepute." Although Welch didn't singlehandedly bring down McCarthy, he did serious damage, showing him for what he was, and wary Republicans backed away.

The Army-McCarthy hearings gave congressional investigations a bad name. By some accounts, the 1973 Watergate hearings redeemed them. Broadcast live for two weeks, the hearings reached millions of American homes daily. Paired with hard-hitting newspaper coverage, they had an impact. Before the hearings, polling showed that 31 percent of Americans considered the Watergate break-in a serious matter. After the hearings, 53 percent shared that view.

The times were different, of course. There was bipartisan support for upholding national institutions and the rule of law; the Senate voted unanimously to create a select committee to investigate Watergate. The mainstream media was suspect to some, but it hadn't been under siege for years as part of a sustained attack on facts and truth. And bald-faced lies by politicians, when exposed, carried a cost.

Left unexposed, such sins can drift into irrelevance, a desired outcome for some. This was the logic of the lukewarm response to government lapses in security during the burning of Washington in 1814—the last time the Capitol suffered a mass attack before January 6. The British savaged the city, torching the president's house (now the White House) and the Capitol. According to one account, a British soldier gloried in the burning of the House while standing on the speaker's chair.

Once the British took their leave, questions abounded: Why wasn't the city defended? Who was at fault? After a couple of months of investigation, the committee tasked with answering these questions issued a voluminous report—but placed no blame. It was little more than a "chronicle," complained Senator Daniel Webster. It had "done nothing that it was asked to do." Not long thereafter, the report was tabled and forgotten. Why? As one congressman later noted, "The House could no more discuss than the committee pronounce upon transactions implicating so many marked personages, and such conflicting evidence of occurrences unquestionably disgraceful to the government and the country." Better to consign the matter to "merciful oblivion" than to implicate men of power.

We face a similar challenge today. Some members of Congress are leery of an investigation and its implications, but their silence comes at great cost. Although accountability won't singlehandedly end our current crisis, its absence virtually guarantees more of the same. With no clear line in the sand, the attack on democracy will continue, unchecked and empowered, with the worst yet to come.

America's Third Reconstruction

PENIEL E. JOSEPH

Boston Globe, August 22, 2022

The House Select Committee investigation into the January 6, 2021, attack on the U.S. Capitol is difficult to comprehend without understanding the history behind the nation's three periods of Reconstruction.

American history since the end of the Civil War has involved a struggle between reconstructionists and redemptionists for the nation's very soul. There is the America that might be proudly called reconstructionist, home to champions of racial democracy, and there is the America that might best be characterized as redemptionist, a country that yearns for a past where structures of domination embedded racial, class, and gender hierarchies through an allegiance to white supremacy.

The First Reconstruction established a set of competing political and cultural norms and frameworks—reconstructionist and redemptionist—regarding Black citizenship, the virtues of Black dignity, and the future of American democracy.

Reconstructionists fervently believed in a vision of a multiracial democracy. They sought, through the Reconstruction Amendments (the Thirteenth, which abolished racial slavery; the Fourteenth establishing birthright citizenship; and the Fifteenth, which extended voting rights to Black men), the Freedmen's Bureau, the federal entity set up to ease the transition from slavery to freedom for four million Black Americans. Ultimately the goal was to institutionalize economic reparations through land redistribution, to elect those committed to citizenship and dignity for all people, and the reunification of families separated by slavery.

Redemptionists championed public policies that stripped Black voting and citizenship rights. Across the former Confederacy, states passed laws, adopted codes, and enacted policies that made it difficult for Black people to exercise the rights of citizenship and almost impossible to enjoy personal dignity.

The Second Reconstruction spanned the civil rights movement from the 1954 Supreme Court decision in *Brown v. Board of Education of Topeka* to Martin Luther King Jr.'s assassination in 1968. And we have come to the Third Reconstruction, the period from the election of Barack Obama through the recent Black Lives Matter protests and the January 6 attack and hearings.

The violence that erupted at the nation's capital on January 6, 2021, contains a direct throughline across three periods of Reconstruction in America—from the eruption of white racial terror campaigns that stalled the First Reconstruction to the white violence that greeted Black people who tried to vote, eat at restaurants, swim at beaches, travel on buses, or stay in hotels during the Second Reconstruction to our current discontents.

The January 6 hearings find their historical analogue in the congressional hearings investigating anti-Black violence by the Ku Klux Klan that unfolded in January 1871. Back then, elected officials listened to harrowing testimony of Black Americans victimized by racial terror amid a political backlash aided and abetted by local officials who collaborated with racial terrorists and a federal government that frequently ignored violent massacres quaintly referred to as "outrages." For example, in 1868, a white mob in Camilla, Georgia, killed numerous Black people in the state's southwestern region, marking the beginning of the end of African American political power in rural areas.

In 1873, more than one hundred Black people were massacred in Colfax, Louisiana, by white Fusionists (an alliance of conservative Republicans and Democrats) after an all-Black militia had taken over the courthouse to protect the duly elected Republican government from white mob violence. The passage of the Enforcement Acts gave the federal government new powers to curtail anti-Black violence by allowing for the federal prosecution of terror groups such as the Ku Klux Klan, which the Grant administration used sparingly before ultimately abandoning the cause of Black citizenship.

The split screen interpretations of January 6's meaning for American democracy by Republican and Democratic Party officials reflect debates, conflicts, and divisions that can be traced back to the convulsive world built in the aftermath of the Civil War and legal and policy decisions that continue to impact Americans only vaguely aware of this history.

By the twentieth century, redemptionists, who lost the war, had decisively won the peace. They mainstreamed a false vision of a white supremacist American history—popularized in the novel *The Klansman* and the films *Birth of a Nation* and *Gone with the Wind*—that justified anti-Black violence as the cost of a national reunion. This early iteration of the contemporary cultural wars was rooted then, as now, in long-standing racial divisions centered around contested legacies of capitalism and democracy.

But America's Second Reconstruction transformed the social compact for Black folk, and the legacies from this period still reverberate nationally. From President John F. Kennedy through President Barack Obama, the civil rights era institutionalized a fragile national consensus that supported the struggle for Black citizenship and dignity as a political and moral good.

In retrospect, Americans experienced a fifty-year period of national consensus on racial justice between JFK's June 11, 1963, racial equity speech before the nation and the June 25, 2013, *Shelby v. Holder* decision, which gutted the Voting Rights Act. The era was a hinge moment in American history.

Donald Trump's ascent to the White House did more than tip the scales in favor of redemptionists. Trump's victory shattered the national consensus forged in the civil rights era, which helped to launch a new era of voter suppression using tactics that recalled two earlier periods of Reconstruction. Before Trump, figures as disparate as Martin Luther King Jr., Hillary Clinton, Richard Nixon, Michelle Obama, and Ronald Reagan had all expressed public support for and fidelity to a civil rights movement. Unmoored from the public embrace of Black equality that marked the nation's forward-looking stance since the Second Reconstruction, America lost its way.

The public testimony on display throughout the course of the January 6 hearings offers evidence of the depth and breadth of our collective detour away from the multiracial democracy that made the Obama presidency possible. The mob that rampaged through barricades, bludgeoned Capitol Police officers, and defiled the Capitol illustrates Reconstruction's complex legacy. The scenes recalled the organized white violence in Wilmington, North

Carolina, in 1898, when white supremacist recruited state military troops, private militia, and local police to spearhead a massacre that killed dozens of Black men, including some of the city's leading citizens; drove thousands into the frigid woods in a desperate search for survival; and reimposed bigoted Democratic Party leadership that disposed of the interracial Fusionist government that brought together Black Republicans and white populists.

The Capitol attack offered demonstrable proof that the clash between reconstructionists and redemptionists is continuing in the twenty-first century. But the redemptionist efforts to overturn a presidential election, ban the teaching of Black history in schools, and suppress Black voters is not all of who we are. On November 10, 2021, 123 years after the Wilmington massacre and coup d'état, the city finally buried Joshua Halsey, a Black man who in 1898 had been shot fourteen times and buried in an unmarked grave. The forty-seven-year-old father of four never lived to see an America not threatened by his dreams. But perhaps his descendants might. Wilmington's shame is America's shame, and our efforts to bring truth, justice, and reconciliation to these dark parts of our history—as the January 6 hearings have attempted to do—underscore how a nightmare can still be a dream.

Militia Groups Were Hiding in Plain Sight on January 6; They're Still Dangerous

KATHLEEN BELEW

Washington Post, January 6, 2022

As we mark the anniversary of the January 6 assault on the Capitol, and as different judicial processes attempt to deliver their various forms of accountability, we still lack an adequate understanding of one of the day's imminent dangers: the threat of militias to American democracy.

The invasion of the Capitol is best understood as the collision of three streams of right-wing activity: the Trump base (itself containing a range of extremism), the QAnon movement, and white power and militant right groups. This third segment—although probably smaller than the others involved that day—was highly organized, connected, outfitted with tactical gear and weapons, and well trained. These activists often led the charge, and they were the first to breach the Capitol. Their own ideology, which descends from decades of violent white-power organizing, reveals them to be dangerous, intent on the destruction of democracy and the propagation of race war.

One question that stands out: Why did these activists who attended the January 6 action mostly not wear Nazi and Klan gear or carry symbols of organized white power? Why, instead, did they show up in yellow and black, in paramilitary gear, and carrying militia flags?

I have spent sixteen years researching the history of white-power and militia activity. One consistent attribute of the militant right is that it is fundamentally opportunistic: White power and militia groups tack not only to the prevailing winds that point toward likely scapegoats, but also toward cultural acceptability. Even before January 6, these groups received information (in the form of condemnation from politicians and other sources) that outright racist mobilizations would not curry favor with a broad group of supporters. Although the groups donned white polo shirts and khakis in Charlottesville for the Unite the Right rally in 2017, most politicians condemned their openly racist and anti-Semitic message. This point was surely driven home later by the federal jury verdict in *Sines v. Kessler*, which in November found the organizers of the Unite the Right rally liable for $25 million in damages.

But militias, as the scholar Joe Lowndes has documented, have not received similar condemnation. Even before January 6, militia groups appeared regularly in semi legitimate and legitimate settings, at antimask actions and even at Black Lives Matter protests.

And on the day of the electoral vote count, even groups that espouse white power ideology cloaked their most offensive symbols.

This shows us, once again, that January 6 was meant as a recruitment and radicalization action—an attempt to raise awareness about the militant right and bring people into the fold. For this reason, the pressing work ahead will be clarifying the threat that extralegal militias pose to people, governance, and institutions.

To be sure, some militias are distinct from some forms of white power activism. But there is a large degree of overlap, and militias are not separate enough to earn the label of neutrality. The word "militia" holds a special place for many Americans because it calls back to our Constitution, to our early history, and to the role of militias in the Revolutionary War. However, those militias were incorporated into National Guard units in the early twentieth century. The militias on the scene now do not have a clear lineage to the well-regulated bodies enumerated in the Constitution. Furthermore, as the legal scholar Mary McCord has shown, all fifty states ban such groups in one way or another.

The militias we face today are, quite simply, extralegal, unregulated, private armies.

These private armies often show up saying they are there to "keep order." They have provided private security for politicians (like the First Amendment Praetorian members who have accompanied former Trump adviser Mike Flynn, and the Proud Boys with Roger Stone).

They have also done things like detain protesters at the behest of police in Portland, Oregon.

They have provided security for a GOP event in Colorado Springs, and then showed up there and elsewhere to pack school board and town council meetings to pressure local communities about to ban racially inclusive curriculums and masking.

Not only does this range of activity show that militias remain active as a local and national political threat, but too often, these groups do real harm with real casualties. Consider the Unite the Right rally in Charlottesville: part of the reason police did not protect counterprotesters who were beaten and killed was because, according to then-Governor Terry McAuliffe, they were far outgunned by militias.

Extralegal private armies prevented police from ensuring safety? That is neither law nor order.

Extralegal private armies intimidated local communities to defy public health guidance in schools? That is neither health nor safety.

And extralegal private armies attempting to stop us from teaching and learning our own history? That is a direct attack upon our knowledge of civics, sense of community, and the very tools we will need to overcome the threat of January 6. This is to say nothing of the larger canvas of police violence and white supremacy, the problem of veteran and active-duty military participation in militia and other militant right groups, and the clear and present danger these groups pose to democracy. A recent report from *BuzzFeed News* documented at least twenty-eight elected officials with ties to the Oath Keepers.

Without an understanding of what a militia is, someone might believe joining such a group is an exercise related to patriotism, or heritage. Instead, it is downright terrifying: elected officials with ties to extralegal, unregulated private armies.

This is a threat to Americans, to our democracy, and to our institutions. Part of the work of the courts, the January 6 Commission and our public conversation about the day is to understand the degree of culpability in our halls of governance that allowed the riot. But part must also be to reckon with violent militia groups themselves, and with the continued presence of extralegal private armies across the nation.

January 4, 2022

HEATHER COX RICHARDSON

Letters from an American, January 5, 2022

Late this afternoon, the House Select Committee to Investigate the January 6th Attack on the U.S. Capitol asked Fox News Channel personality Sean Hannity voluntarily to answer questions about his communications with former president Donald Trump and Trump's White House chief of staff Mark Meadows in the days around the January 6 insurrection.

In their letter requesting the conversation, committee chair Bennie Thompson (D-Miss.) and vice chair Liz Cheney (R-Wyo.) revealed evidence that Hannity was deeply involved with White House matters, acting not as a member of the press but as an advisor. In fairness, by his own account Hannity has always been a political operative. In August 2016, he told Jim Rutenberg of the *New York Times,* "I'm not hiding the fact that I want Donald Trump to be the next president of the United States." After all, he said, "I never claimed to be a journalist."

Treading carefully to reassure Americans that the members of the committee are not interested in undermining the independence of the press, the January 6 committee asked Hannity to comment on "a specific and narrow range of factual questions." The committee made it clear that "our goal is not to seek information regarding any of your broadcasts, or your political views or commentary." They reiterated their desire only to understand the facts at issue, and they appealed to Hannity's love of country and respect for our Constitution to ask him to "step forward and serve the interests of your country."

The committee's letter specified that they had seen a number of Hannity's texts, all of which were eye-popping and which revealed that Hannity was acting as an inside member of Trump's team. On December 31, 2020, he texted Meadows: "We can't lose the entire WH counsels office. I do NOT see January 6 happening the way he is being told. After the 6 th. [sic] He should announce will lead the nationwide effort to reform voting integrity. Go to Fl[orida] and watch Joe mess up daily. Stay engaged. When he speaks people will listen."

On January 5, the night before the insurrection, Hannity "sent and received a stream of texts," including the message: "Im very worried about the next 48 hours." The committee noted that the counting of the certified ballots was scheduled for 1:00 on January 6, so why was Hannity worried about the next forty-eight hours?

Hannity appears to have talked with Trump on January 10 and was concerned with what he heard. He texted Meadows and Representative Jim Jordan (R-Ohio), saying, "Guys, we have a clear path to land the plane in 9 days. He can't mention the election again. Ever. I did not have a good call with him today. And worse, I'm not sure what is left to do or say, and I don't like not knowing if it's truly understood. Ideas?"

The texts reveal that Hannity saw his role not as a newsreader, but rather as a member of the White House team, protecting the president, and Hannity's participation in the conversations means that none of them can be considered privileged.

Hannity is apparently being represented in this matter by Jay Sekulow, a lawyer on Trump's legal team, rather than lawyers from the *Fox News Channel*. While Sekulow has indicated he will object to the committee's invitation on First Amendment grounds, the fact that the *Fox News Channel* seems to be standing back suggests that the corporation does not see the committee's invitation as a First Amendment case involving freedom of the press and in fact might well be concerned that one of its lead personalities is connected to an event that should have been reported to the FBI.

Blaming the "total bias and dishonesty" of the select committee, Trump today canceled his press conference planned for January 6.

July 12, 2022

HEATHER COX RICHARDSON

Letters from an American, July 13, 2022

Today the House Select Committee to Investigate the January 6th Attack on the U.S. Capitol held its seventh public hearing. This one focused on how former president Trump summoned right-wing extremists to Washington, D.C., on January 6, 2021, in a last-ditch effort to overturn the 2020 election.

Committee members reiterated that Trump's advisors had told him repeatedly that there was no evidence for his claims that the election had been corrupt. Again and again, White House officials demanded of Trump's allies that they produce evidence of their accusations of fraud, and they never produced anything, choosing instead to attack those demanding evidence as disloyal to Trump. There is no doubt that Trump knew quite well there had been no fraud that would have changed the outcome of the election, and that he was lying when he continued to insist the election had been stolen.

Representative Liz Cheney (R-Wyo.), the committee's cochair, began the hearing by noting that there had been a change recently in those defending Trump's actions, as it has been established that Trump's advisors had made it clear to him the election was not stolen. From arguing that he didn't know the election was fair, they have switched to suggesting that he was misled by bad actors like John Eastman, who articulated the plan to have Vice President Mike Pence refuse to count certain of Biden's electors, or Trump lawyer Sidney Powell.

But, Cheney said in words carefully calculated to infuriate the former president: "This is nonsense. Trump is a seventy-six-year-old man. He is not an impressionable child. Just like everyone else in this country, he is responsible for his own actions. . . . [He c]annot escape responsibility by being willfully blind."

The focus in today's hearing was on Trump's actions between December 14, when the Electoral College met in all fifty states and in the District of Columbia to certify the ballots that elected Democrat Joe Biden, and the morning of January 6, when Trump pointed the rally-goers at the Ellipse toward the U.S. Capitol.

With the electoral votes certified for Biden on December 14, even then–Senate majority leader Mitch McConnell congratulated Biden publicly on his election, and numerous White House officials, including White House counsel Pat Cipollone, Attorney General Bill Barr, White House chief of staff Mark Meadows, and White House press secretary Kayleigh McEnany, either urged Trump to concede or began looking for new jobs on the assumption the White House would change hands on January 20.

But Trump and his allies looked to January 6, when those electoral votes would be counted, as the last inflection point at which they might be able to overturn the election.

On December 18, 2020, four days after the electors met, Trump's outside advisors, including lawyers Rudy Giuliani and Sidney Powell, former national security advisor Michael Flynn, and Patrick Byrne, former chief executive officer of Overstock, got access to the White House through a junior staffer and met with

Trump. They brought an executive order that had been drafted on December 15, the day after the electors had certified the votes for Biden. It called for Trump to order the Defense Department to seize state voting machines, and it appointed Powell as special counsel to investigate voter fraud, giving her broad powers. They wanted Trump to implement it.

Cipollone got wind of the meeting and crashed it about fifteen minutes in. Over the next six hours, White House officials and the Trump team members who insisted the election was stolen faced off, exchanging personal insults, accusations of disloyalty to the president, even challenges to fight physically. Cipollone, White House lawyer Eric Herschmann, and their team demanded evidence to support the theories Trump's outside team insisted were true. In turn, the outside team repeated conspiracy theories and accused the others of being wimps: Powell told the committee the White House team all should have been fired, and Giuliani told the committee he told them all they were "a bunch of p*ssies."

In the end, Trump was convinced not to follow the direction of the outside advisors. But he didn't take the advice of those officials telling him to concede, either. Instead, shortly after the meeting broke up, Meadows walked Giuliani out of the White House to make sure he didn't sneak back into Trump's company. Then, at 1:42 on the morning of December 19, Trump reiterated to followers that the election had been stolen and that there was no statistical way that he could have lost.

Then he typed the words: "Big protest in D.C. on January 6. Be there, will be wild!"

Immediately, his most loyal supporters recognized this tweet as a call for armed resistance. "Trump just told us all to come armed," one tweeted. "F*cking A, this is happening."

Far-right media, including Alex Jones of InfoWars, amplified Trump's tweet with calls to violence. The committee introduced testimony from a former Twitter moderator who said: "We had not seen that sort of direct communication before" in which Trump was speaking directly to supporters and inciting them to fight. After the December 19 tweet, it was clear, the person said, "not only were these individuals ready and willing, but the leader of their cause was asking them to join him in this cause and in fighting for this cause in D.C. on January 6 as well."

Supporters wrote comments like: "Why don't we just kill them? Every last democrat, down to the last man, woman, and child?" and, making the link between Trump's determination to stay in office and white supremacy: "It's time for the DAY OF THE ROPE! WHITE REVOLUTION IS THE ONLY SOLUTION!"

As Trump continued to post about January 6 on Twitter and continued to insist he had won the election, militias, white supremacists, and conspiracy theorists began to work together to coordinate an attack on the Capitol. The Proud Boys and the Oath Keepers, along with other extremists groups, worked with Trump allies to plan the attack. Those allies included Michael Flynn and Patrick Byrne.

Another ally was Trump confidant Roger Stone, who talked both to the Proud Boys and the Oath Keepers "regularly." The committee got access to an encrypted chat of the "Friends of Stone," or "FOS," including Stone, Oath Keepers leader Stewart Rhodes, Proud Boys leader Enrique Tarrio and agitator Ali Alexander. Kelly Meggs, the leader of the Florida Oath Keepers, spoke directly with Stone about security on January 5 and 6. Stone was guarded on January 6 by two Oath Keepers who have been indicted for seditious conspiracy.

Stone was also close enough to the Proud Boys to have "taken their so-called fraternity creed required for the first level of initiation to the group." The clip of that oath shows him saying: "Hi, I'm Roger Stone. I'm a Western chauvinist, and I refuse to apologize for creating the modern world."

The committee made it clear that Trump deliberately created the crisis on January 6. Katrina Pierson, organizer of the Ellipse rally, was so worried about Stone, Jones, and Alexander as speakers at the rally, that she talked to Meadows on January 2 about them, warning a fellow organizer that Trump "likes the crazies." On that same day, Meadows warned his assistant Cassidy Hutchinson that things could get "real, real bad" on January 6.

The committee produced evidence from a number of emails and tweets from Trump and other organizers saying that after the rally, Trump would urge attendees to march to the Capitol, undercutting the argument that the move was spontaneous. In fact, it was long planned.

The committee also introduced evidence that the White House coordinated with members of Congress to encourage the "Big Lie" and to fight the election results. Representative Mo Brooks (R-Ala.) set up a meeting between members of Congress (and one member-elect) on December 21, with the subject line: "White House meeting December 21 regarding January 6." That meeting included Trump, Pence, Meadows, Giuliani, and ten representatives: Brian Babin (R-Tex.), Andy Biggs (R-Ariz.), Matt Gaetz (R-Fla.), Louie Gohmert (R-Tex.), Paul Gosar (R-Ariz.), Andy Harris (R-Md.), Jody Hice (R-Ga.), Jim Jordan (R-Ohio), Scott Perry (R-Pa.), and recently elected Marjorie Taylor Greene (R-Ga.).

This sheds light on Trump's comment to officials from the Department of Justice in which he asked them just to say the election was corrupt and leave the rest up to him and the Republican congress members. A number of those involved in the meeting later asked for presidential pardons.

Some in Trump's inner circle were excited about what was to come. Phone logs show Trump spoke to confidant Steve Bannon at least twice on January 5. After the first call, Bannon said on his podcast that "all hell is going to break loose tomorrow." "It's all converging and now we're on . . . the point of attack." "I'll tell you this: it's not going to happen like you think it's going to happen. . . . It's going to be quite extraordinarily different and all I can say is strap in."

That night, as supporters gathered at Freedom Plaza to hear the extremist speakers who had been excluded from the event of January 6, including Roger Stone, Michael Flynn, Alex Jones, and Ali Alexander, Trump was in a notably good mood for the first time in weeks. Stone told the crowd it was in an "epic struggle for the future of this country between dark and light, between the godly and the godless, between good and evil. And we will win this fight or America will step off into a thousand years of darkness."

In his speech the next day at the Ellipse, Trump insisted on inserting attacks on Pence and urging his supporters to "fight like hell [or] you're not going to have a country anymore." That rhetoric, former Trump campaign manager Brad Parscale told Pierson, had caused people to die.

Today's hearing ended with the testimony of former Oath Keepers social media manager Jason Van Tatenhove, who warned that the Oath Keepers are a danger to the country, and a Trump supporter, Stephen Ayers, who was not affiliated with any right-wing groups but who stormed the Capitol after Trump told him to. Both of them blamed themselves for being misled by Trump and extremism. Van Tatenhove warned that the danger is ongoing.

As if on cue, Cheney dropped the information that since the last hearing, Trump has tried to reach a witness with a personal phone call. The witness avoided the call and contacted a lawyer instead. This attempt smacks of desperation on Trump's part, as well of isolation: no one would do the dirty job of intimidating a witness for him. The committee sent the information about this attempt, which involves someone the public has not yet seen testify, to the Department of Justice.

More and more, witnesses seem to be siding with transparency and the committee rather than with Trump. Today, Dan Friedman of *Mother Jones* published a tape of Bannon on October 31, 2020, laughing as he explains to a private audience that Trump will "win" in 2020 simply by declaring he won, even if he didn't.

Trump knew that Democratic mail-in ballots would show up in the vote totals later than Republican votes cast on election day, "[a]nd Trump's going to take advantage of it," Bannon said. "That's our strategy. He's gonna declare himself a winner. . . . So when you wake up Wednesday morning, it's going to be a firestorm," he said. "You're going to have antifa, crazy. The media, crazy. The courts are crazy. And Trump's gonna be sitting there mocking, tweeting sh*t out: 'You lose. I'm the winner. I'm the king.'"

And, Bannon continued: "Here's the thing. After then, Trump never has to go to a voter again. . . . He's gonna say 'F*ck you. How about that?' Because . . . he's done his last election. Oh, he's going to be off the chain—he's gonna be crazy."

NOTES:

Brian Naylor, "Read Trump's January 6 Speech, A Key Part of Impeachment Trial," NPR, February 10, 2021, https://www.npr.org /2021/02/10/966396848/ read-trumps-jan-6-speech-a-key-part-of-impeachment-trial.

Bryan Metzger, "Eleven House Republicans Attend a White House Meeting with Trump to Strategize About Overturning the Election Results," Insider, July 12, 2022, https://www.businessinsider.com /house-republicans-white-house-meeting-december-21-2020 -election-2022-7.

Dan Friedman, "Leaked Audio: Before Election Day, Bannon Said Trump Planned to Falsely Claim Victory," Mother Jones, July 12, 2022, https://www.motherjones.com/politics/2022/07/leaked-audio -steve-bannon-trump-2020-election-declare-victory/.

Isaac Arnsdorf and Josh Dawsey, "January 6 Panel Escalates Showdown with Trump over Influencing Witnesses," Washington Post, July 12, 2022, https://www.washingtonpost.com/national-security/2022 /07/12/trump-witness-tampering-jan-6/.

Bob Brigham, "This is Huge: Legal Experts React to Liz Cheney's January 6 Bombshell Claim," Salon, July 12, 2022, https://www.salon .com/2022/07/12/this-is-huge-legal-experts-react-to-liz-cheneys -jan-6-bombshell-claim/.

January 6 Hearings
The Truth May Not Be Enough to Prove Democracy Is Still a Viable Form of Government

HEATHER COX RICHARDSON

Milwaukee Independent, July 26, 2022

The July 21 public hearing by the House Select Committee to Investigate the January 6th Attack on the U.S. Capitol brought to its logical conclusion the story of Trump's attempt to overturn our democracy. After four years of destroying democratic norms and gathering power into his own hands, the former president tried to overturn the will of the voters.

Trump was attacking the fundamental concept on which this nation rests: that we have a right to consent to the government under which we live. Far from rejecting the idea of minority rule after seeing where it led, Republican Party lawmakers have doubled down.

They have embraced the idea that state legislatures should dominate our political system, and so in 2021, at least nineteen states passed thirty-four laws to restrict access to voting. On June 24, in the *Dobbs v. Jackson Women's Health* decision, the Supreme Court said that the federal government did not have the power, under the Fourteenth Amendment, to protect the constitutional right to abortion, bringing the other rights that amendment protects into question. When Democrats set out to protect some of those rights through federal legislation, Republicans in Congress overwhelmingly voted to oppose such laws.

In the House, Republicans voted against federal protection of an individual's right to choose whether to continue or end a pregnancy and to protect a healthcare provider's ability to provide abortion services: 209 Republicans voted no; 2 didn't vote. That's 99 percent of House Republicans.

They voted against the right to use contraception: 195 out of 209 Republicans voted no; 2 didn't vote. That's 96 percent of House Republicans.

They voted against marriage equality: 157 out of 204 Republicans voted no; 7 didn't vote. That's 77 percent of House Republicans.

They voted against a bill guaranteeing a woman's right to travel across state lines to obtain abortion services: 205 out of 208 Republicans voted no; 3 didn't vote. That's 97 percent of House Republicans.

Sixty-two percent of Americans believe abortion should be legal. Seventy percent support gay marriage. More than 90 percent of Americans believe birth control should be legal. I can't find polling on whether Americans support the idea of women being able to cross state lines without restrictions, but one would hope that concept is also popular. And yet, Republican lawmakers are comfortable standing firmly against the firm will of the people. The laws protecting these rights passed through the House thanks to overwhelming Democratic support but will have trouble getting past a Republican filibuster in the Senate.

When he took office, Democratic president Joe Biden recognized that his role in this moment was to prove that democracy is still a viable form of government.

Rising autocrats have declared democracy obsolete. They argue that popular government is too slow to respond to the rapid pace of the modern world, or that liberal democracy's focus on individual rights undermines the traditional values that hold societies together, values like religion and ethnic or racial similarities. Hungarian president Viktor Orbán, whom the radical right supports so enthusiastically that he is speaking on August 4 in Texas at the Conservative Political Action Conference (CPAC), has called for replacing liberal democracy with "illiberal democracy" or "Christian democracy," which will explicitly not treat everyone equally and will rest power in a single political party.

Biden has defended democracy across the globe, accomplishing more in foreign diplomacy than any president since Franklin Delano Roosevelt. Less than a year after the former president threatened to withdraw the United States from the North Atlantic Treaty Organization (NATO), Biden and Secretary of State Antony Blinken pulled together the NATO countries, as well as allies around the world, to stand against the Russian invasion of Ukraine. The new strength of NATO prompted Sweden and Finland to join the organization, and earlier this month, NATO ambassadors signed protocols for their admission. This is the most significant expansion of NATO in thirty years.

That strength helped to hammer out a deal between Russia and Ukraine with Turkey and the United Nations on July 23 to enable Ukraine to export twenty-two million tons of grain and Russia to export grain and fertilizer to developing countries that were facing famine because of Russia's blockade of Ukrainian ports. An advisor to the Ukrainian government called the agreement "a major win for Ukraine." When a Russian attack on the Ukrainian port of

Odesa today put that agreement under threat, U.S. ambassador to Ukraine Bridget A. Brink called the attack "outrageous."

Biden has also defended democracy at home, using the power of the federal government to strengthen the ability of working Americans to support their families. As soon as Biden took office, Democrats passed the $1.9 trillion American Rescue Plan to rebuild the economy. It worked. The U.S. has added ten million new jobs since Biden took office, and unemployment has fallen to 3.6 percent.

That strong economy has meant higher tax revenues that, combined with the end of pandemic spending, have resulted in the budget deficit—the amount by which the government is operating in the red each year and thus adding to the national debt—dropping considerably during his term.

The strong economy has also led to roaring inflation, fed in part by supply chain issues and high gas prices. During the pandemic, as Americans turned to ordering online at the same time that factories closed down, shipping prices went through the roof. In the past year or so, outdated infrastructure at U.S. ports has slowed down turnaround while a shortage of truckers has slowed domestic supply chains. Biden's administration worked to untangle the mess at ports by getting commitments from businesses and labor to extend hours, and launched new programs to increase the number of truckers in the country.

While oil companies are privately held and thus have no obligation to lower their prices rather than pocket the record profits they have enjoyed over the past year, Biden has nonetheless tried to ease gas prices by releasing oil from the strategic reserve and by urging allies to produce more oil for release onto the world market. Gas prices have declined for the past month and now average $4.41 a gallon, down from a high of more than $5 last month.

Last month, on June 25, Biden signed into law the first major gun safety bill in almost thirty years, having pulled together the necessary votes despite the opposition of the National Rifle Association. On July 21, he signed the bipartisan FORMULA—which stands for "Fixing Our Regulatory Mayhem Upsetting Little Americans"— Act to drop tariffs on baby formula for the rest of the year to make it easier to get that vital product in the wake of the closure of the Sturgis, Michigan, Abbott Nutrition plant for contamination, which created a national shortage. The Biden administration has also organized fifty-three flights of formula into the country, amounting to more than sixty-one million 8-ounce bottles.

While we have heard a lot about Biden's inability to pass the Build Back Better part of his infrastructure plan because of the refusal of Republicans and Democratic senator Joe Manchin (W.Va.) to get on board, Biden nonetheless shepherded a $1.2 trillion bipartisan infrastructure bill through this partisan Congress, investing in roads, bridges, public transportation, clean energy, and broadband.

Love or hate what Biden has done, he has managed to pull a wide range of countries together to stand against Russian president Vladimir Putin's authoritarian attack in Ukraine, and he has managed get through a terribly divided Congress laws to make the lives of the majority better, even while Republicans are rejecting the idea that the government should reflect the will of the majority. That is no small feat.

Whether it will be enough to prove that democracy is still a viable form of government is up to us.

Select Bibliography

Belew, Kathleen. *Bring the War Home: The White Power Movement and Paramilitary America*. Cambridge: Harvard University Press, 2018.

Clinton, Catherine. *Confederate Statues and Memorialization*. Athens: University of Georgia Press, 2019.

Cox, Karen L. *No Common Ground: Confederate Monuments and the Ongoing Fight for Racial Justice*. Chapel Hill: University of North Carolina Press, 2021.

Downs, Jim. *Why We Write: The Politics and Practice of Writing for Social Change*. New York: Routledge, 2005.

Foner, Eric. *The Story of American Freedom*. New York: Norton, 1999.

Freeman, Joanne B. *The Field of Blood: Violence in Congress and the Road to Civil War*. New York: Picador, 2019.

Hemmer, Nicole. *Partisans: The Conservative Revolutionaries Who Remade American Politics in the 1990s*. New York: Basic, 2022.

Hinton, Elizabeth. *America on Fire: The Untold History of Police Violence and Black Rebellion Since the 1960s*. New York: Norton, 2021.

Joseph, Peniel. *The Third Reconstruction: America's Struggle for Racial Justice in the Twenty-First Century*. New York: Basic Books, Hachette Book Group, 2022.

Kornhauser, Anne. *Debating the American State: Liberal Anxieties and the New Leviathan, 1930–1970*. Philadelphia: University of Pennsylvania Press, 2015.

Kruse, Kevin M., and Julian E. Zelizer. *Myth America: Historians Take on the Biggest Legends and Lies About Our Past*. New York: Basic, 2023.

Lepore, Jill. *The White of Their Eyes: The Tea Party's Revolution and the Battle over American History*. Princeton: Princeton University Press, 2011.

———. *These Truths: A History of the United States*. New York: Norton, 2018.

McCurry, Stephanie. *Confederate Reckoning: Power and Politics in the Civil War South*. Cambridge: Harvard University Press, 2012.

Novick, Peter. *That Noble Dream: The 'Objectivity Question' and the American Historical Profession*. Cambridge: Cambridge University Press, 1998.

Painter, Nell Irvin. *Southern History across the Color Line*, 2nd Ed. Chapel Hill: University of North Carolina Press, 2021.

Petrzela, Natalia Mehlman. *Classroom Wars: Language, Sex, and the Making of Modern Political Culture*. New York: Oxford, 2015.

Richardson, Heather Cox. *How the South Won the Civil War: Oligarchy, Democracy, and the Continuing Fight for the Soul of America*. New York: Oxford University Press, 2020.

Sturkey, Wiliam. *Hattiesburg: An American City in Black and White*. Cambridge: Harvard University Press, 2019.

Young, Neil P. *We Gather Together: The Religious Right and the Problem of Interfaith Politics*. New York: Oxford University Press, 2015.

Zelizer, Julian E. *Burning Down the House: Newt Gingrich, the Fall of a Speaker, and the Rise of the New Republican Party*. New York: Penguin, 2020.

Zucchino, David. *Wilmington's Lie: The Murderous Coup of 1898 and the Rise of White Supremacy*. Atlantic Monthly Press, 2020.

Permission Credits